Touch
I'm Sick
xxx

Touch Me, I'm Sick

I'm Sick

XXX

The 52 Creepiest Love Songs You've Ever Heard

Tom Reynolds

CHICAGO
REVIEW
PRESS

An A Cappella Book

Cover design: TG Design
Cover images: Supapixx/Alamy (Cassette tape);
    PhotoAlto/Alamy (Tape pulled out of cassette);
    Index Stock/Alamy (Burnt cassette)
Interior design: Tara O'Leary
Illustrations: Stacey Earley

First published by Portrait, an imprint of Piatkus Books, London
This edition published in 2008 by
Chicago Review Press, Incorporated
814 North Franklin Street
Chicago, Illinois 60610
ISBN 978-1-55652-753-1
Printed in the United States of America
5 4 3 2 1

For Denise, Erin, Kara, and William

Contents

ACKNOWLEDGMENTS

The author would like to thank Albert DePetrillo for his keen editorial guidance and creative vision, Denise Dwyer for her excellent assistance, Judy Piatkus for the green light, and everybody at Piatkus Books.

Thanks also to Gunnard Reynolds, Jeanne Reynolds, and Bruce Reynolds.

Special thanks to Jack Grisham for his gracious permission to reprint the lyrics to "Code Blue."

INTRODUCTION

Love and Its Discontents,
or the Ballad of Melissa Etheridge

IN 2005 I published a book entitled *I Hate Myself and Want to Die: The 52 Most Depressing Songs You've Ever Heard*. Writing it involved listening to hours of gloomy music while drinking a lot and mumbling to myself. I selected fifty-two songs, shredded most of them viciously, then spent several weeks cranking old KC and the Sunshine Band hits if only because they have the word "sunshine" in their name.

My depressing list included titles by the Cure, Bruce Springsteen, Loretta Lynn, Evanescence, Barry Manilow, and Billie Holiday. I had no songs by the Smiths, however, which some critics felt was like leaving the Resurrection out of the New Testament. (The truth is I'd initially written a chapter on the lachrymose band from Manchester but later had to withdraw it for reasons too tedious to explain.) In short, the absence of Smiths songs along with my arrogant U.S.-centric writing style offended enough people to warrant a sequel.

Although I could've written volumes on the subject, I opted against another analysis of depressing songs since nobody was going to cover any more Zoloft prescriptions. I needed another musical subgenre to explore, but which one? Fifty-two cheeriest songs? Most boring? Worst uses of a rapper on a Jennifer Lopez single? After much arguing and a few thrown glasses of Guinness, we decided this book would examine the world's creepiest love songs. It would be entitled *Touch Me, I'm Sick* from a song by Mudhoney, an unwashed Seattle grunge outfit who were contemporaries of Nirvana, whose song "I Hate Myself and I Want to Die" inspired the title of the last book. It seemed like the perfect follow-up, a volume about obsession to complement one about depression.

Then the trouble started.

It was easy to find depressing songs for *I Hate Myself*. Friends, colleagues, and total strangers inundated me with long lists of morbid tunes by artists varying from Nick Drake to Nick Cave, Radiohead to Portishead, Nine Inch Nails to Three Doors Down. But when I asked the same people for suggestions of creepy love songs, I received either bemused silence or "Every Breath You Take" by the Police. I might as well have asked for fifty-two best Freddie Prinze Jr. films.

This lack of response puzzled me at first, but later I realized it made sense. A song can make us depressed for all sorts of reasons, be they lyrical, sonic, or thematic, or because Phil Collins recorded it (while I relish the melancholy of Richard Thompson, I'll step in front of trains to avoid Collins' "In the Air Tonight"). Music can drain our spirits even if it has no lyrics at all; listen to anything by German drone-synth weirdoes Tangerine Dream and you'll understand. But for a love song to creep us out requires that we pay close attention to the lyrics and, seriously, who has the patience for *that* nowadays?

But the more I thought about it, the more I suspected denial was the main reason. Nobody could think of any creepy love songs because they remind us of something we don't want to admit: love today is creepy.

Clinically, love suffers from *creepinization*, defined as the onset of creepiness over any cherished institution. Take love at first sight, for example. It used to be that a naked cherub would hit us with an arrow. Today the implants have to look real. Love once inspired sonnets, plays, and novels. Now it inspires "Smack That" by Akon. Creepinization has replaced all of love's romance and mystery with reality dating shows and Brangelina. Love used to come with flowers. Now it has a publicist.

Popular culture has its filthy paws all over it. We've been

bludgeoned by Paris Hilton sex videos and twenty years of Madonna's hoo-hoo (if a woman gets naked and there's no camera around to film it, did nudity take place?). Young people today learn about love from pop culture, the one thing that always gets everything wrong. Seemingly passionate behavior in TV and movies is borderline psycho in real life. In the 1989 film *Say Anything*, there is the famous scene in which John Cusack stands outside Ione Skye's window blasting Peter Gabriel's "In Your Eyes" on a boom box. It's considered one of the most romantic moments in cinema history. But try it for real and you'll be arrested for playing an eighties song in public.

Modern romance has turned into a cruel spectator sport not seen since the Romans featured Christian & Lion Night at the Coliseum. I for one can attest to this. I once worked on *Elimidate*, the reality TV dating show. It was basically *The Bachelor* only with one-fifth the cast and ten times the inebriation. The premise involved a guy going on a date with four girls (or a girl with four guys), then sending them away one by one throughout the half-hour episode. At the end the guy chose one girl as his new love, the relationship lasting as long as the credit rolled. *Elimidate* showcased many of today's dating rituals, including body shots, three-way make-out sessions and the verb "conversate" (as in "the girls and I sat at a table so we could conversate"). After three seasons and 450 episodes, I came away with two realizations about contemporary relationships: 1. Love is creepy, and 2. 70 percent of women born after 1983 are named Nicole.

Today love has divided itself into four distinct types: ephemeral, conditional, narcissistic, and whacked.

- **Ephemeral:** Love with the shelf life of week-old cod. Slow courtship is usurped by the immediacy of MySpace, AIMs, and blogs. Couples hook up, marry, and split in the time it takes to download porn. People get dumped via text message: **K-fed: We're thru. Get the fk out. Brtney.**

- **Conditional:** Love built on a convoluted set of requirements, clauses, rules, regulations, and agreements. Marriage vows come with terms as long as a Proust novel. Divorces are filed because the socks don't match the tie.

- **Narcissistic:** Love based on an extreme infatuation with the self. Celebrities refer to themselves in the third person, the most obnoxious form of name dropping ever conceived. YouTube features people's contribution to the visual arts, i.e. posting video clips of them chugging beer bongs and lip-synching to Lenny Kravitz.

- **Whacked:** Love that's obsessive, grasping, bitter, shallow, warped, or involves any TV reality show starring a celebrity couple.

Love songs have changed accordingly. While I normally abhor cliches unless I can make money from them, the old chestnut "They don't write 'em like that anymore" certainly holds true when it comes to romantic expression. The most vivid examples were found in odes, a form of lyric poetry heavy on feeling and light on prenuptial agreements. The nineteenth-century English poet John Keats was renowned for his odes, his most famous being "Ode on a Grecian Urn." If you haven't read it, it's a poem about a vase (poetry often addresses inanimate objects like trees and Pete Doherty). Anyway, "Ode on a Grecian Urn" contains an extraordinary series of couplets about love in its third stanza:

> *More happy love! More happy happy love!*
> *Forever warm and still to be enjoyed,*

Forever panting, and forever young;
All breathing human passion far above,
That leaves a heart high-sorrowful and cloyed,
A burning forehead, and a parching tongue.

Few writers today could pull off verses like these without milking the irony or adding words that rhyme with Nantucket. Alas, odes aren't written much nowadays as contemporary poets prefer "free verse," so named because nobody gets paid to write it. Besides, someone who writes odes is considered an odist. Try putting it on a resume.

Early popular songwriters like Rodgers and Hart, Frank Loesser, Bertolt Brecht, and Irving Berlin, masters whose work Rod Stewart would later eviscerate, employed a nuance in their lyrics not often found today. Let's compare:

Someday,
When I'm awfully low
And the world is cold,
I will feel a glow just thinking of you
And the way you look tonight.
Jerome Kern and Dorothy Fields,
"The Way You Look Tonight"

With:

I want to fuck you like an animal
Nine Inch Nails, "Closer"

That's not to say every pre–Second World War songwriter was swirling a martini glass while penning the latest Bing Crosby hit in his Manhattan loft. In 1937, while Harold Arlen and E. Y. Harburg were writing "Over the Rainbow" for Judy Garland, the legendary (and allegedly cursed) blues musician Robert Johnson* was sitting under a tree somewhere scribbling the following lyrics:

> *Now you can squeeze my lemon*
> *Till the juice run down my leg,*
> *Baby, you know what I'm talkin' about*
> from "Traveling Riverside Blues"

These lines would show up more than thirty years later on Led Zeppelin's "The Lemon Song," proving that not every suggestive lyric comes with an expiration date. Likewise, other blues giants like Charley Patton recorded songs about a woman's "sweet jellyroll" and having a "hot dog for your bun" (jazz pioneer Jelly Roll Morton did not get his moniker from a bakery item). It was one of the cheekier ways songwriters could drop a sexual reference into a song without describing how many D cells the average vibrator requires. This is why America was unprepared for Japan's attack on Pearl Harbor in 1941; it was too distracted by all the double-entendres flying past it.

I'm no nostalgia fiend. Cole Porter wrote the inane "Let's Fall in Love" with its litany of copulating crustaceans, while Gus Kahn and Walter Donaldson's "Makin' Whoopee!" was silly the day it was conceived. But the all-must-be-revealed approach to songwriting is very much a by-product of current times. Today's love songs are corrupted by gore and nakedness. One looks for sublime romantic ballads and winds up with Melissa Etheridge, an artist whose love songs contain more cannibalism metaphors than chord changes: she is to creepy love songs what Tesla was to electricity. Ms. Etheridge is a longtime member of the CHAI (Chicks with Acoustic Instruments) movement, along with Sarah

---

* Johnson was either poisoned by a jealous bartender or dragged off to hell after selling his soul to the devil, depending on your taste for apocrypha.

McLachlan, Jewel, Joan Osborne, Alanis Morissette, Paula Cole, Suzanne Vega, and the rest of the Lilith Fair army who came to prominence during the late nineties. Although earlier artists like Joan Baez, Judy Collins, Laura Nyro, and the brilliant Joni Mitchell explored introspective songwriting, the CHAIs have eclipsed them by raising the confessional bar so high that only an emotionally tortured pole-vaulter could clear it.*

While the CHAIs bared their souls, the nineties "boy bands" unctuously wooed the teenage heart. There was a time when you couldn't enter a Foot Locker or wait at a stoplight next to a Mazda with a blasting radio without hearing their Anglo gushings. Since I followed boy bands as closely as I do Peruvian llama farming, I wrongly assumed one group was responsible for "I Want it That Way," "Bye Bye Bye," "The Hardest Thing," "All or Nothing," and any number of high-fructose radio ballads with the word "loving" in the title. Turns out all these songs were performed by four different groups, being the Backstreet Boys, 'NSYNC, 98 Degrees, and O-Town. Whatever individuality they possessed ended at their monikers. Musically they hewed to a formula so narrow it resembled a vein: either hip-hoppy dance tracks with a lot of bloodless grunting or oozing love ballads that you could pour on French toast. Their members even looked alike, right down to the one guy with the razor-thin beard that appeared to be drawn on with a Sharpie. They starred in TV specials, created clothing lines, took acting gigs, and dated Disney ingenues like Hilary Duff and Lindsay Lohan (prompting cat fights even better than their music). All the while, their love songs kept the same glossy polish and faux-emotional heart yanking

---

* One aspect of CHAI songs is that you can usually find an angel in their lyrics. In recent years, angels have been under exclusive contract to crystal-reading karma-obsessed pagan types who can draw spiritual meaning from watching pigeons crap on a car window. That's all well and good but with so much strife in the world today, don't angels have better things to do than to come flitting into the chorus of every other Tori Amos song?

that they always had. Still, I cannot fathom how the Backstreet Boys managed to sell eighty-three million albums. What monstrous alien uber-pod birthed eighty-three million people eager to snap up a CD with "As Long As You Love Me" on it?

But while pushing the envelope and heavy marketing play a big part in the swell of creepy love songs, we cannot forget simple unawareness: we're just not paying attention. Consider the afore-mentioned "Every Breath You Take" by the Police, which Sting wrote about the dissolution of his first marriage. While many music fans recognize it as the national anthem of stalkers, this is apparently lost to the estimated two thousand people who play it every year at the funerals of loved ones (it is allegedly the ninth most popular song featured at memorial services). There are also the two thousand additional clueless wonders who play it at their weddings (see page 27).

So how does one recognize a creepy love song? First, it must be dissected to fully understand its creepiness; it's like doing an autopsy except the corpse has a copyright. Creepy love songs often aren't as obvious as their depressing counterparts. While even a flea can hear the grimness in "Heaven's a Lie" by Lacuna Coil, most people have never noticed the homicidal intent behind the Beatles' "Run for Your Life." After careful study I've found fifty-two creepy love songs, some of them good-creepy, others bad-creepy. All can be heard within the maw of LimeWire, satellite radio, or any karaoke bar run by Lucifer. Most come with music videos available on YouTube. They're grouped into ten different categories, as follows:

Hopelessly Devoted to You: Stalker tunes are the most com-mon and obvious of creepy love songs. They disguise themselves as examinations of impassioned love but are just plain nutso.

Touch Me, I'm Sick: Remember that stammering dweeb who text-messaged "You're my universe" to your mobile phone? He's now a songwriter.

I Want to Fly Like an Ego: Narcissistic songs in which artists brag about how great they are in an obnoxiously over-the-top manner. These anthems to self-love often feature singers referring to their selves in the third person.

Love's Just Another Word for I Want to Eat Your Liver: Devoted to the women artists of the CHAI movement, known for their emotionally confessional songwriting.

I'm Not Bitter, I Just Wish You'd Die, You Miserable Pig: Remember that chick you broke up with because she was a psycho? She's now a songwriter.

All in the Family: Too sick to even imagine, these incest-themed love songs detail an unnatural carnal attraction to a blood relative, including but not limited to . . . Mom. There are more of them than you know.

Death Becomes Us: Yes, even necrophilia has been taken for a spin by songwriters. This section looks at corpse-happy songs where a couple's love is eternal even when one of them is wasting away. Literally. Again, there are more of them than you know.

Those Freaking Butterfly Songs: This section examines four of the creepiest love songs ever written in which butterflies have starring roles.

Little Ditties About Oral Sex and Masturbation: No explanation necessary.

Perfect Storms: The most sickening and egregious creepy love songs ever forced upon the listening public.

With any book of this kind, there are going to be glaring omissions that readers will find outrageous. Also, my critical analyses of various performers are entirely subjective. While I can state without question that uranium-235 is an isotope, I can't prove scientifically that Fergie's "Fergalicious" blows chowder. There's no equation showing that Sophie B. Hawkins's "Don't Stop Swaying" is one of the creepiest (and worst) songs ever written. These are simply my base opinions with which some people won't agree. Finally, I actually like several of the songs I've included in this book. They just happen to be creepy as hell.

HOPELESSLY DEVOTED TO YOU

OBSESSION

Words and music by Michael Des Barres and Holly Night
Performed by Animotion
Released 1985 (No. 6 in U.S., No. 5 in UK)

IT MAY seem a little obvious to begin this book with a song entitled "Obsession," but I have an ulterior motive, namely a reconsideration of eighties music. It's important to note that eighties songs differ from songs recorded during the 1980s. The early work of U2, REM, and the Police is not eighties music. To truly experience eighties music, one must endure Thompson Twins, Missing Persons, Human League, Berlin, Simple Minds, and other groups who built their sound around the polyphonic synthesizer, an eighties-era analogue keyboard with an uncanny knack for recreating the sound of farting meerkats.

Oblong and button-heavy, the polyphonic synthesizer infected 68 percent of pop songs released during the 1980s, including the clanging sounds heard during the chorus of Simple Minds' zeitgeist hit "Don't You (Forget About Me)." "Do-nnn't you . . . (clang, claaaaanng) . . . forget about me . . . (CLAAANNNG!!) . . . don't, don't, don't, don't . . ." Polysynths were ubiquitous during the Thatcher era because they allowed rudimentary piano players who couldn't master "Heart and Soul" to join bands and ruin rock music. Watch any old A Flock of Seagulls, Haircut 100, or Jesus Jones video and you'll see a guy with geometric hair banging away on a polysynth with the dexterity of someone trying to close an overstuffed suitcase. Nothing conjures up an eighties flashback more than the cheesy sound of a polyphonic synthesizer; it's the *Miami Vice* rerun of musical instruments.

This brings us to the electronica stalker hit "Obsession." Originally written and recorded in 1983 by British vocalist

Michael Des Barres and singer Holly Night, the L.A.-based band Animotion released their version in 1985, which reached the Top 10 in both the U.S. and the UK. True to the eighties music template, it showcased a flatulent polysynth and a unique pairing of a male and female co-lead vocalist, unique in that neither one of them could sing.

THE SONG

The lyrics to "Obsession" are your standard crazed psycho/kidnapper sort, but what separates this song from its stalker brethren is two vocalists, Bill Wadhams (Stalker A) and Astrid Plane (Stalker B) who trade verses throughout. There's a squishy robotic drum machine that opens it up before a polysynth smacks its way into the backing track, jabbing out chords that sound like a Labrador barking at a squirrel in a tree. Right away, the eighties flashback begins: Rubik's Cube, Mount St. Helens, Chernobyl, Molly Ringwald with a career.

"You're an obsession", Wadhams sings first in a strident tenor, "I cannot sleep . . . ," declaring that he won't be defeated despite their lack of equality and balance, something apparently no stalker wants. Then Astrid takes over and states the objective more clearly, "I will have you, yes I will have you," adding how she will collect and capture him like a butterfly. This suggests a strange premise: they're two stalkers stalking each other.

When the chorus kicks in, the first thing you notice is that it sounds exactly like the verse section save for the addition of guitar/funk bass accents straight off a Duran Duran track, which only exacerbates the eighties contact high you're already experiencing (look, there's Judd Nelson, Diana Spencer, and Boy George invading the Falkland Islands). "You're my obsession," the two wail together, demanding who they should be so they can sleep with each other. Talk about two peas in a paranoia pod.

As the song continues, the stakes are raised while New Coke hits the market. "I feed you, I drink you," declares Wadhams, adding how she can't leave and there's no alternative. I've seen enough reruns of *CSI* to recognize the modus operandi of a deranged stalker, but the whole template is compromised when Astrid comes back in. For some reason, she sees danger afoot and notes that his affection *is not what it seems*. Now I'm confused. Who's stalking who and to what degree? Meanwhile, the barking polysynth pummels you with more eighties apparitions: Pac-Man, stonewashed jeans, Iran-Contra, mutant turtles, hair resembling a Trojan helmet.

After a second spin through the chorus, the verses close on the two of them openly acknowledging that they're both pretty far gone. "My fantasy has turned to madness," Wadhams confesses, which is apparent since he rhymes it with badness. He whimpers about his lack of control while Astrid repeats her declaration of collecting him like a butterfly, etc. The song concludes with a faux-metal guitar solo that rocks somewhat but doesn't supersede the grating polysynth chords that pound throughout. It ends, the Berlin Wall falls, all is right in the world again.

WHY IT'S CREEPY

Besides having two vocalists, many aspects of this song come in twos: the number of minutes it took to write it, the number of notes in the melody, the number of weeks it was a hit before people got sick of it, etc. Lyrically "Obsession" borrows practically every psychotic thought a stalker possesses and puts it on display over a grating synth bed while expecting the listener to go along on the ride. I'm mystified as to why Animotion felt compelled to have two people sing a song with lyrics like this since it's obviously written from one maniac's point of view. Maybe they had to give Astrid something to do. Actually, there should be a legal clause drawn up which states that anyone named Astrid shouldn't be allowed to sing. Granted, there aren't many vocalists named Astrid but the ones I've heard, namely Astrid Survanto, Astrid Duncan, Astrid Breck, and Astrid Plane of this song, aren't cut out to be vocalists. Perhaps they were hired to sing simply because they were named Astrid. It certainly looks more exotic on a marquee than Sheryl or Melissa.

"Obsession" kept Animotion as frozen in the eighties as any number of hit songs did all those other bands that put more time and effort into wardrobes and bad video shoots than into figuring out how to write a song that wasn't built on a polysynth. No wonder grunge took over.

EVERY BREATH YOU TAKE

Words and music by Gordon Sumner, AKA Sting
Performed by the Police
Released 1983 (No. 1 in U.S., No. 1 in UK)

WHEN I started researching this book, most people came up blank when I asked them for creepy love song suggestions. The only tune anyone could think of (and I mean the *only* one) was the Police's "Every Breath You Take." Well, I'm no dummy, so I put the song on my list. I soon discovered that it's one of the top ten most played songs at weddings and funerals. So I took it off the list. Then I found out the song was Sting's bitter reaction to the end of his first marriage. It went back on the list. Then I heard the Puff Daddy version. I took it off the list and you know why. Finally the Police announced that they were reuniting for a world tour; the song would be everywhere once again. I put it back on the list.

Personally, I've always enjoyed "Every Breath You Take," but couldn't imagine why people would play it at their wedding. How dense do you have to be not to notice the lyrics? I can understand if I told someone "I have six monkeys in hats who waved to Scarlett Johannson" and they thought *Wow, he had hot monkey sex with that waif Scarlett Johannson*. But "Every Breath," no way. It's about a stalker ferchrissakes.

THE SONG

While I like "Every Breath You Take," I've also heard it so many times over the years, I've no need to listen to it again. I can even draw it:

```
        5 duhn                        5 duhn
   3 duhn    6 duhn  8 duhn   3 duhn      6 duhn  8 duhn
  2 duhn  4 duhn   7 duhn    2 duhn  4 duhn    7 duhn
1 duhn                       1 duhn
```

This is the song's guitar figure using notation without actual notes (think of them as bars on your cellular). Police guitarist Andy Summers plays it throughout the entire song without once stopping to ask for directions. This is not a dig. Ask any experienced guitarist to play it for four minutes straight and *not make a mistake*. Odds are, he'll choke.

Sting then enters with his Newcastle burr and adopts the persona of a stalker planning . . . whatever it is stalkers plan. This would normally be my cue to paraphrase the lyrics, except that it feels odd. See, every other word in this song is "every" and almost every line is "every (noun) you (verb)." He's obsessed with every breath, every move, every bond, every step, along with her days and words and games. Whatever it is, "I'll be watching you."

As for the chorus, there isn't one. Perhaps stalkers dislike choruses—I'm not sure. Whatever the reason, it's not needed as Sting declares "you belong to me" and how much his heart hurts with "every step" she takes, probably while fleeing.

The next stanza is where the whole "let's play this at our wedding" idea turns preposterous. To wit: "Every vow you break, every smile you fake." The song's bridge sets aside the sinister pulse for a plaintive wail of grief. Summers slams ringing chords while Sting/stalker dreams of her face while feeling lost because she's gone forever. I'm pretty sure these lyrics have always been in the song, so if any engaged couples reading this still want to play "Every Breath You Take" at their wedding, all I can say is "Good luck" (if any readers are urging their engaged friends to play it, you're sick bastards).

The hypnotic guitar figure returns and Sting repeats his desire to be everywhere so he can see everything she's doing, including watching the vow she breaks and the smile she fakes (yes, it's repeated twice just in case the groom doesn't catch it the first time). The track fades to a disquieting silence. OK, time to throw the bouquet.

WHY IT'S CREEPY

Anyone with half an eardrum can fathom the disturbing theme of "Every Breath You Take." Remember, it was the first tune people thought of when I asked for creepy song ideas, so it's secured its place as one of the darkest love songs of all time. "Every Breath" is still regularly played on radio (Sting reportedly earns approximately $2,000 *a day* in royalties from it) yet as ubiquitous as it is, one never gets sick of hearing it. Beneath its pathology and criminal voyeurism is a ballad of utter loneliness. The lyrics ingeniously mimic the elliptical thoughts that fly around an obsessive's brain in mad loops, while the arpeggio-driven music pushes everything forward.

"Every Breath You Take" remains the Police's biggest-selling single, which is ironic since it's the most un-Police-sounding song the group ever recorded. The group based its sound on an innovative mix of reggae polyrhythms, syncopated bass, and ambient chiming guitar. When "Every Breath" hit No. 1 worldwide in 1983, though, it struck critics as too simple, too elementary, the lyrics sounding like a things-to-do list. And the rhymes! Good God, there's "take," then "make," then "break." Most of them missed the point of the song. God knows the wedding party did.

RUN FOR YOUR LIFE

Words and music by John Lennon
Performed by the Beatles
Released 1965 (no chart position)

I HAVE a theory regarding Beatles songs: whoever sang it wrote it (unless it was Ringo, in which case Paul wrote it but was too embarrassed to sing it). I know Mop Top fans hold the Lennon-McCartney collaboration sacred but Lennon would've rather joined the Tory party than have anything to do with "Ob-La-Di, Ob-La-Da" or "Blackbird." Likewise, McCartney lent nary a grace note to "Come Together" or "Across the Universe." This divisiveness was more apparent after the mid-sixties, when Beatles songs became more stylized, eccentric, and occasionally dark. Although I've always loved the Fab Four and know their music pretty well, I decided to seek out an authentic Beatles scholar to help in my quest to find the band's creepiest love song.

One thing I discovered about Beatles scholars is that many of them hate Paul McCartney. In their circles John Lennon is held up as a deity while Sir Paul is loathed. I find this odd but who am I to argue? After much searching, I tracked down a Beatles scholar whose Web site was JOHN_IS_GOD_PAUL_IS_CRAP.com. I emailed him and received an Instant Message response written in that bizarro AIM language everyone uses:

> BS: Thank u for yr interest in music of the Beatles. If you want 2 luk at crepiness in the Beatles catalogue, luk no further thn that hack Paul McCrtney. He's bin riding on John Lennon's legcy 4 yrs.
>
> TR: *What about Yesterday? Hey Jude?*
> *Let It Be? For No One?*

BS: LOL! John wrote those. McCartney dint write a single song 4 the Beatles cept Revolution No. 9 + Ballad of John and Yoko. BTW, John wrote all of Grge Harison's songs too cept Blue Jay Way and those wiggy Injun sitar things. LOL!

I certainly didn't know any of this. I was curious since the Beatles song I was interested in was the sinister "Run for Your Life" from the 1965 album *Rubber Soul.*

BS: Ah, yeh, Run 4 Yr Life. It's in D maj. John strumed a Martin D-18 acuostic, Grge used a Gretsch w/ considerble rust on the 2nd string, and Ringo playd a 3-peice Ludwig drm set equiped w/ Slingerland ride+crash cymbals. The hi-hat pedl wuz sligtly tarnished n th snare drum had a strippd tension nut. LOL!
TR: *How could you possibly know all that?*
BS: Im a Beatls scholr. Oh, whats-hiz-name played bass. Whatever. LOL!

I haven't a clue how he knew all this. I guess this is what makes Beatles scholars stand out among average music nerds like myself. But I was more concerned with the lyrics to "Run For Your Life." John Lennon once claimed in an interview that it was his weakest Beatles song. I asked the scholar about the song's opening line, "I'd rather see you dead, little girl, than to be with another man." It's lifted directly from the old Elvis Presley hit "Baby, Let's Play House."

BS: True. But thats McCrtnys fault. He orderd John 2 steal lyrics frm a Presly song.

Again, this was new to me. But the lyrics that follow are all Lennon's. We hear how he's a wicked guy with a "jealous mind."

He warns the girl that she has to "toe the line." The chorus sums up his chauvinism quite succinctly: the girl has to run for her life and hide her head in the sand. If he catches her with another man, he'll kill her. I asked the scholar if Lennon didn't sound controlling and obsessive.

> BS: Thats Ringo he wuz talkin about. Ringo wuz psycho about grls.
> *TR: Really? I thought Ringo was the most normal laid-back guy in the Beatles.*
> BS: Blame Paul. LOL!

I was beginning to understand his rationale, which many Beatles scholars hold to: John Lennon never wrote a bad song. I suspect this is why the Lennon-McCartney attribution is so useful to them because any weak aspects to a Beatles song can automatically be blamed on McCartney, even if he had nothing to do with it. The last stanza to "Run for Your Life" is the creepiest, as Lennon sings how he means everything he's told her including he'd rather see her dead. I asked the Beatles scholar about it.

> BS: It jus shows Paul's hostlity. Like, the last line about rathr seein her ded. Thats actualy Paul sayin that 2 the girl.
> *TR: I thought you said it was Ringo.*
> BS: It wuz Ringo in 1st part. The rest is Paul. LOL!
> *TR: Wow. You sure know a lot.*
> BS: Im a Beatls scholr.

WHY IT'S CREEPY

When you consider the passage of time along with the Beatles' amazing ratio of superior songs to weak ones, "Run for Your Life" sounds more hostile today than it did over forty years ago. Besides being misogynistic, the song is also very thrown together.

Lennon admitted that he wrote it in a hurry to fill out the rest of the *Rubber Soul* album and disliked it ever since. I challenged the scholar with this point.

BS: Tru, John nevr likd the song. N-fact, he hatd it evn b4 he wrote it.

TR: How do you hate a song before you write it?

BS: Again, Pauls fault. Whn they came up short 4 Rubber Soul, he told John, I want u 2 write n offnsive song bout thretening to kill a GF. You have 2 hate it th whole time youre writng it.

TR: Wow. I didn't know that.

BS: BTW Did u know John wrote all the songs 4 Paul McCartney and Wings too?

TR: Really? Band on The Run? Live and Let Die? Junior's Farm?

BS: All by John. Except Silly Love Songs. LOL!!

TR: Boy, you sure know a lot.

BS: Im a Beatls scholar.

YOU'RE ALL I NEED

Words and music by Nikki Sixx
Performed by Mötley Crüe
Released 1987 (No. 83 in U.S., No. 23 in UK)

POISON, WARRANT, Ratt, Slaughter, W.A.S.P., Cinderella, White Lion, Skid Row, Pretty Boy Floyd, Dokken: these cretins of crapola were all part of the eighties "hair band" scene that was thankfully eclipsed when Nirvana came out. Hair bands did more to destroy rock 'n' roll than any censorious parents' group ever could, and all of them should be sentenced to twenty years in purgatory listening to Sabbath and Zeppelin until they go, "Oh, now I get it." Seriously, why didn't Ratt and Poison just hook up and form Ratt Poison?

It was Mötley Crüe that occupied the summit of this hirsute heap. Its members spent all their time exploiting hair band cliches like Playmate girlfriends, Sodom-and-Gomorrah antics, and skinny skinny arms protruding from Lycra shirts. This left them too busy to learn how to write a decent rock song, and instead they filled their albums with boring sped-up riffs and atonal screaming. If they were bad at writing headbangers, they were even worse at "power ballads," those lumbering faux-sentimental tracks that sounded like a rhino walking to the gallows (and got a surprising amount of airplay). One of the worst is the Crüe's creepy ballad "You're All I Need," about a guy languishing in prison after murdering his girlfriend in a jealous rage. The title is apropos since after one listen, I immediately thought, "Geez, this is *all* I need."

THE SONG

Someone alert the descendants of Bartolomeo Cristofori, the

inventor of the piano. They must file suit because their patriarch's noble instrument can be heard in "You're All I Need," bombarded by nasal fuzz guitars, clomping bass, and Tommy Lee's this-is-boring-when-can-I-solo drums. In one of his most execrable vocal performances, Vince Neil wail-whines about being in a padded prison cell as he recalls how the blade of his knife "sliced you apart." We can assume he's killed his girlfriend for betraying him, i.e. she had her breast implants removed. Now locked up in the wing reserved for psychotics and incompetent tenors, he says how he shed his "blood" and "tears" for her (what, no sweat?) because he "loved you cyanide," the first time a poison has ever been used as an adverb.

The song's chorus is one of those everyone-sing-along contrivances that only a teenage glue-sniffer would fall for. "You're all I need," Neil cries, adding that in order to set her free, he had to kill her. I'd accuse Mötley Crüe of sophistry if I didn't have to explain to them what it means. He sums it up neatly about how he loved her so much but "you didn't love me."

As harmonized guitar fills fly around like wounded parrots, we're pretty much ready to ditch this joint. OK, you killed her because you loved her but hated her because she didn't love you. I get it, can we go home now? But no, there's more to hear, for apparently there was an ulterior motive for committing blonde-icide: "We finally made the news," Neil sings. Why couldn't he just put out a sex tape like everybody else?

The chorus repeats as the odor of model plane cement fills the room. We hear the "set you free by killing you" drivel again, and the last stanza reveals how he figured she was only napping because she never opened her eyes. (I guess the knife stuck into her ribs wasn't enough of a clue.) After a paint-by-numbers guitar solo from Mick Mars (who's a better musician than this), the chorus takes us out of the building, where the fresh air snaps us back to reality and we realize we'll never get the four and a half minutes of our lives we spent listening to this song back again.

WHY IT'S CREEPY

If some readers think I'm a prude who's objecting to the subject matter of this song, that's incorrect. The murder ballad is a standard part of music literature, dating back to the Renaissance with its songs of bloodied swords and patricide. A murder ballad only works as a tragic morality tale (Lefty Frizzell's "The Long Black Veil") or an experiment in dark humor (Warren Zevon's hilarious "Excitable Boy"). "You're All I Need" is neither. It's simply a fatuous attempt at being topical while trying to stay within the narrow parameters of the hair band power ballad. The numerous references to obsessive love ring hollow, and the sniggering comment about "making the news" doesn't work as irony. What creeps me out about this song is that it doesn't serve its subject matter and instead feels like crass exploitation of the theme of jealousy and murder. There's a very thin area in which one can work to create a powerful murder ballad, and when you sport a teased haystack coif and jet-black mascara, and have transcripts from the Salem witch trials tattooed on your torso, it's a little difficult for anyone to take it seriously. No wonder people got sick of power ballads. If you liked this song back when you were sixteen, fine. If you still like it twenty years later, you need to quit your job working at the copier store.

Although its members have had various fallings-out, Mötley Crüe continues to tour, as do other reunited hair bands like Poison, Warrant, and Dokken. They still play the old songs, still throw up devil signs, still scream, and still use flash pots and smoke machines. Oh, and they still suck.

WHERE THE WILD ROSES GROW

Words and music by Nick Cave
Performed by Nick Cave with Kylie Minogue
Released 1995 (No. 11 in UK)

I'VE JUST watched the music video for the Nick Cave and Kylie Minogue duet "Where the Wild Roses Grow." Not to give away anything, but Nick Cave lives up to his surname and caves in Kylie Minogue's head with a stone. Hmm, interesting. In Australia, they take their dance-pop stars and hit them with rocks. In America, they give them their own reality shows and cast them in movies. Talk about being behind the curve.

"Where the Wild Roses Grow" is one of the many cheery tracks on the 1995 album *Murder Ballads* by Nick Cave and the Bad Seeds. Cave wrote "Wild Roses" in the style of a traditional murder ballad like "Tom Dooley," right down to its quaint lyrics and the Scottish-Irish conceit of its music. To date, the song is the biggest-selling song of gloomy Nick's career, and arguably his creepiest. According to a 1996 magazine article, it was Cave's incongruous idea to have Australian pop star Kylie Minogue duet with him on "Wild Roses" after hearing the supposedly "innocent" way she sang her hit "Better the Devil You Know," which, he insisted, contained some of pop music's "most violent and distressing lyrics." For readers unfamiliar with "Better the Devil You Know," the most distressing-sounding lyric in the entire song is "better the devil you know."

THE SONG

"Where the Wild Roses Grow" opens with a small string ensemble playing an eighteenth-century musical intro while Kylie dons a twentieth-century dress with spaghetti straps and steps into the meadow as the sun backlights her. In a whispery voice, she sings the song's chorus, how everyone calls her the Wild Rose even though her name is Eliza Day. She has no idea why people prefer to call her the former. Maybe Nick knows. "Her lips were the color of roses," he sings in a (very) unsteady sub-baritone. They're the same color as the roses that grow near the river, "all bloody and wild." From the first day Nick saw her singing that distressing "Devil You Know" song, he knew she was the one.

The song's parlor-room strings slither about moodily as Kylie explains how they first met, when he tapped on her door and entered her room. She nervously trembles and cries but Nick holds her close and calms her. He would be "my first man," she sings as he wipes off the tears that "ran down my face." So this is how he first asked her out? Just walk into her house, scare the hell out of her, and then put her in a bear hug while singing out of tune? To think I always spent twenty minutes rehearsing a phone call that started with, "I don't know if you remember me but . . ." What was I thinking?

After the chorus, the two meet up for a second time. "I brought her a flower," Nick intones while sounding more like Lou Reed with each passing bar of music. He asks her if she knows where the wild roses grow. She doesn't. She doesn't even know why everyone calls her the Wild Rose. Then Nick asks her if she'll "give me your loss and your sorrow?" Remember, this is only their second date together. I'd still be explaining away why I drive a six-year-old Ford Escort. But his monotone voice proves irresistible to her and she nods, yes, I will give you my loss and my sorrow. See you tomorrow.

The chorus again. Her name's still Eliza Day yet everyone calls her the Wild Rose. I don't know about you but this would make me paranoid as hell.

Now, it's their third day together. "He took me to the river," Kylie sings, as he shows her the wild roses and they kiss. Now the date turns bad. Really bad. The last thing she hears is him muttering and she looks up to see him holding a rock in his hand.

Finally, Nick concludes the tragic tale, singing how he kissed her goodbye because "all beauty must die." As she lies dead in the water, Nick (the big softie) kneels down and puts a rose between her teeth.

WHY IT'S CREEPY

Among the many unsettling things about this song, including the doom-laden storyline and the muted tragic string music, is the pathological motive for why the girl gets killed. The only clue we get is at the end, when he says how all beauty must die. This kind of atavistic jealousy is common in murder ballads, where an obsessed man feels the only way he can possess the woman he loves is by killing her. The song is a stark example of how it transpires. As a recording, though, "Wild Roses" teeters perilously between being serious art and twisted camp, if only because of Nick Cave's shaky singing (seriously, he's barely in tune). There is a 1996 clip of Cave and Minogue doing a live performance of "Where the Wild Roses Grow" on Australian TV's *Top of the Pops*. While Kylie sings wonderfully, an awkward Nick is so badly out of tune, it's embarrassing.

Because of the surprising popularity of "Wild Roses," Kylie Minogue's career was boosted greatly among critics who'd previously dismissed her as a featherweight pop diva. She delivers a very nice performance and looks stunning in the song's disturbing music video, where viewers can see her dead in the water as a huge snake crawls across her lifeless body. As for Cave, his limited baritone works fine in dark Berlin-heavy art rock songs, but give him a song with a defined melody and he's a drunk on a tightrope. I'd say his singing is probably what kills Kylie in the song. The rock in his hand is just theater.

INVISIBLE

Words and music by Christopher Braide,
Andreas Carlson, and Desmond Child
Performed by Clay Aiken
Released 2004 (No. 9 in U.S.)

FOR ME, singles released by *American Idol* finalists are like the latest models from Hyundai: I'm sure they work but I don't fucking care. And while network execs grovel at the feet of *Idol's* creators, workaday musicians would prefer it if they all died under an avalanche of unsold Taylor Hicks CDs. What's the point of honing your craft and developing a following when the entire music industry has turned into a high-concept karaoke contest?

My big issue with *American Idol* is that the pool of ten finalists is always the same: a felon, a skank, a couple of babes, a virgin, one genuine talent, three people who think Aretha Franklin began her singing career in *The Blues Brothers*, and the why-is-he-still-left guy. During the show's second season, Clay Aiken seemed to adopt each persona (save the first three), depending on what episode it was and whether it involved singing Journey songs. His face-off with Ruben Studdard for the *Idol* crown was slightly surreal, like watching Rocky and Bullwinkle on Open Mike Night. Aiken's second-place finish turned out to be an asset, however, granting him underdog status and the adulation of pubescent girls and grandmothers alike. Wholesome and sunny, Clay even had the perfect name; you could mold him into anything.

The guy would've flown right past my radar if it hadn't been for my friend Willie, a professional musician. We were on the phone one day when I mentioned I was looking for creepy love songs.

"That Clay Aiken song 'Invisible' is sorta creepy," he said. "I think he wants to be invisible so he can get close to some girl."

Hmm, I thought, *a creepy Clay Aiken song* . . . I got ahold of "Invisible," gave it several listens, and streamed the music video, filmed on Hollywood Boulevard, off the Web (note to video producers: homeless teenagers are generally not Clay Aiken fans). The next day I called Willie. The following is an approximate transcription of the conversation that ensued.

THE SONG

"Willie, it's Tom. You were right. That song *is* creepy."

"What song?"

"Y'know, 'Invisible' by Clay Aiken."

"Oh. Right."

"I listened to it ten times."

(Long pause.) "Why?"

"To better understand Clay's mind-set. Like, it starts off with two acoustic guitars, piano, and string synth. They play pop-folk chords while Clay is following this chick around. He's too afraid to talk to her so she doesn't notice him."

"Um, OK."

"But he's Clay Aiken. Y'know, the Clay Man. Every girl's achin' for Aiken."

"Did you just call him the Clay Man?"

"So anyway, he's asking 'whatcha doin' tonight' and wishes he could be a fly on her wall. Isn't that weird?"

"I guess."

"The drums come in and he's wondering if she's alone or if she's got the hots for somebody else. Clay hopes he can breathe her into his life. She doesn't even know he's alive, the poor bastard."

"Listen, I was just heading out."

"Don't interrupt, I'm getting to the chorus. It's one of those soaring hooks that sound like the Goo Goo Dolls going through puberty."

"I have no idea what you just said."

"But this is where it gets creepy. Clay wishes he were invisible just so he can watch her in her room. Did you know that? Imagine an invisible Clay Aiken skulking around someone's room while she's getting undressed."

(No response.)

"Then the Clay Man gets aggressive. He wants to be 'invincible' so he can 'make you mine tonight.' So that's his strategy: sneak into this girl's room unseen, then turn into an unstoppable force so he can ravish her."

(No response.)

"The second verse is all about Clay following this chick around in public. He calls out to her but she doesn't hear him. I'm guessing if you're invisible, it affects your ability to speak."

"Do you need me to call someone?"

"'I keep tracing your steps,' he sings. Clay wants to know every move she makes, every thought she thinks. Then wham, it's back into that leap-out-of-a-flaming-building chorus: 'If I were invisible . . .' He thinks being invisible would make him the smartest man in the world, or something like that. Then there's the bridge."

"Look, I really think you should—"

"It's not a very good bridge. It doesn't have the same catapult effect as the chorus. Plus, it's lyrically stupid. He's complaining how 'you don't even see me.' How can she? He's invisible. I mean, twenty seconds earlier he was saying how smart he was about being invisible, now he's whining about it. No wonder Simon Cowell made fun of him. The chorus returns one more time with the obligatory vocal layering until the fade. That's the whole song, transparent protoplasm and all."

WHY IT'S CREEPY

"Dude, do you realize you just spent the last ten minutes lecturing me about a Clay Aiken song?"

"It's not like it's a bad song, Willie. It's a little below his range in the verse sections, but the chorus is catchy in a sing-along kind of way. I like the double-track acoustic guitars and it sounds like they used a real drummer."

"Yeah, but—"

"Still, it doesn't negate how a song like this is so much more disturbing when you consider who's singing it and what his motivation is. Everyone saw Clay Aiken as the nice polite kid on *Idol* who made Aaron Carter look like Marilyn Manson. But now he's this shape-shifting obsessed voyeur. I mean, would you want an invisible Clay Aiken in your bedroom?"

"Why would Clay Aiken be in my bedroom?"

"It's not that he's in your bedroom, it's that he's invisible in your bedroom. If he was visible, you could just tell him, 'Hey, Clay Aiken, get the hell outta my bedroom.'"

(Dial tone.)

PRETTY WHEN YOU CRY

Words and music by Jon Crosby
Performed by VAST (Visual Audio Sensory Theater)
Released 1998 (no chart position)

SINCE THE mid-1990s there's been an influx of musical acts described as someone's "brainchild." According to *Webster's*, a brainchild is an *original* plan or idea attributed to a single person or group. At one time you had to come up with $E=MC^2$ or invent a working time machine before you could earn a brainchild credit. Now you can get one just for forming a band. You shouldn't but you can.

Literally all brainchild groups have a control freak. In fact, *he's* the group. He adopts a non sequitur name for himself like Nine Inch Nails, Badly Drawn Boy, Aqualung, or He Who Steals Carrots Frightens the Hamster. He scores a major-label deal with his homemade demos on which he plays most if not all the instruments. He hires a full band (which drives him nuts) so he can tour. He releases a few albums then gets into a fight with his label because they demand commercial songs. He becomes independent and releases his next albums under his creative control. They aren't as good as the ones he did with the demanding major label. He gives guarded interviews to fawning music journalists and continues touring with a constantly changing group of backup musicians.

Now let's meet VAST, an acronym for Visual Audio Sensory Theater and the "brainchild" of California musician Jon Crosby. For his career bio, see above. For a description of his creepy love song about emotional sadism "Pretty When You Cry," keep reading. You'll learn why a track that I otherwise admired because of its structure, dramatic musical arcs, and solid engineering also riled me completely because of my own personal baggage (which is unfair and unprofessional, I know).

THE SONG

"Pretty When You Cry" begins with a sinister Moog bass pattern and drum accents that suggest this song is up to no good. Crosby adopts the persona of a narcissistic passive-aggressor who dominates the band, er, girl in his life while shielding himself with disingenuous apologies. He sings to her how she's "made of my rib bone, baby," using the old Adam's rib dodge to set her up so she can bite the apple later. He remarks that he can't tell where her lust for him ends and her love begins. It would seem he's worried she'll switch out the lust part of their relationship with love and he'll be required to have a conversation with her. This leaves less time to sample monk chants from imported CDs (inside joke, but you know you get it).

As for the chorus, well, you hear it a lot in this song. "I didn't want to hurt you," he repeats thrice, "but you're pretty when you cry." Variations on this lovely disclaimer appear throughout. He takes a brief break to seduce the moon, however, saying that she's given him permission. Before you can say waxing gibbous, the moon is "losing her virginity" along with her will to compromise. So then, is the girl the moon? Is the moon the girl? Is the girl mooning Keith Moon? Oh, you brainchild types . . .

"I didn't want to fuck you," he repeats thrice, except that she's pretty "when you're mine." I don't know what to make of this line other than I'm wondering how he was able to say it to her without getting his cajones hacked off. "I didn't really love you," he adds (thrice). He just thinks he's "pretty when I lie."

If we recap, we see that he intentionally hurt her so she'd cry, screwed her to exact control and pretended to love her because he enjoyed lying. Oh, and he admits it to her. Now he's shamelessly throwing samples of Gregorian wailing, African flutes, and assorted schoolgirl choruses into the song's cynical stew. There's some feedback guitar and squealing synth noises. Finally, Crosby slaps us with his final qualifier. If the girl only knew how he loved her, he sings, she'd run away. So the reason he treats her like crap is that it "makes you want to stay."

More chanting, more feedback. "I didn't want to hurt you," Crosby sings as the song builds to a climax before ending on a drone at the fade. He brushes himself off, walks past the girl's weeping form on the floor, and exits the room.

WHY IT'S CREEPY

Although he's not as nihilistic as Trent Reznor, Jon Crosby pretty much follows the lone tortured artist schematic with his dark songs about emotional turmoil. His best may be "Touched," a powerful song about lost love that appeared on his 1998 debut album. It's so good I'm surprised it wasn't a hit. As for "Pretty When You Cry," it's not as good as "Touched" but is still an intense song with a hypnotic groove. Obviously its creepiness is in the character's callous, almost pathological, manipulation of the girl he torments for his own gratuitous needs. It's very real, very effective, and very unsettling to listen to.

The question is, is "Pretty" good-creepy or bad-creepy? I'll admit my judgment is impaired on this one. See, the guy Crosby portrays in the song is exactly the kind of prick I heard about from weeping girls who cried on my shoulder back in college. In any random week, I'd get a Cathy, Roxie, Kay, whoever boo-hooing about some jerk she was dating and how he didn't want to see her tonight, he's out with his buddies, he's always a shit to her. Finally they'd peck me on the cheek, thank me for listening, I was a swell guy, then go back to him the next day. I dare say I'm not the only guy who endured this, where we lose the cute girl to the arrogant bastard who yells at the valet and won't tip. But since I don't want to be biased against Mr. VAST, I'll just say give the song a listen and see if you don't recognize somebody you know who has a gorgeous girlfriend for no logical reason.

CREEP

Words and music by Thom Yorke, Jonny Greenwood, Ed
O'Brien, Colin Greenwood, Phil Selway, Albert Hammond,
and Mike Hazlewood
Performed by Radiohead
Released 1993 (No. 34 in U.S., No. 7 in UK)

ONE DAY I got curious and Googled songs with "creep" or
"creepy" in the title to see what was out there. I found hundreds
of titles by such musical giants as Guffey, Smeer, Lagwagon,
Munkey Juice, Jag Offs, and my personal favorite I Can Lick Any
Sonuvabitch in the House (note to group: you will never make it
with that name but it still made me laugh). This was how I
rediscovered Radiohead's "Creep," a song about a self-loathing
loser who follows around a girl he's too afraid to speak to (call it
"passive stalking"). It made a splash in the U.S. charts in 1993
while vaguely resembling the 1974 Hollies hit "The Air That I
Breathe." As their first and biggest-selling single, "Creep" put the
critically acclaimed Radiohead on the map while causing them
way more anxiety than it should have.

There are five members in Radiohead, but if you look at the
writing credits above for "Creep," you'll notice seven names
there. That's because the last two, Albert Hammond and Mike
Hazlewood, who were the writers of "The Air That I Breathe,"
were given copublishing credits on "Creep." This is something
Radiohead willingly offered and while it was a noble gesture, I
haven't a clue why they did it. The only thing "Creep" and "Air"
have in common is a slow tempo and similar chords in their
respective verse sections. But many listeners were led to think
"Creep" and "Air" were the same song because of their identical
use of a stylized chord progression, stylized in that it's wrong.

Allow me to get technical. Both songs are in different keys, "Creep" in G major, "Air" in B major. Regardless, a song's chord progression is based on the intervals between the chords, and this is where an overlap occurs, albeit temporarily:

Creep—G/B/C/C minor (repeats through entire song)

Air—B/D#/E/E minor (doesn't repeat through entire song)

With both songs, the interval between the first two chords is a major third, while the interval between the second and third chords is a half step. Finally, the fourth chord is a minor version of the third chord in both songs. Got it? Therefore, both are the same except in a different key (if you're bored, and I don't blame you, skip the next paragraph).

What makes this progression distinctive is that according to the Dead White Guy rules of harmony, the second and fourth chords in both songs are technically wrong. The second chord should be minor, not major, because of its relationship to the first chord. The fourth chord being minor is also wrong, unless you're using it as a "pivot" chord to modulate to a different key, which doesn't happen in either song (good God, I'm boring myself).

Suffice to say, one of the great things about music is that you can break the rules as much as you want and screw what Bach established four hundred years ago. You also cannot copyright a chord progression and besides, it's near impossible to write a song with a chord progression that hasn't been used before (if you have, I'll assume you're Frank Zappa and you faked your death). Radiohead just happened to write "Creep" using a chord progression that had been used thirty years earlier in a Hollies song. Their respective melodies are slightly similar but not overtly so and beyond that, the twain don't meet at all. "Air That I Breathe" also contains a bridgelike second-verse section plus a chorus that sound nothing like "Creep." Therefore, Your Honor, Thom Yorke and company were needlessly generous.

THE SONG

Now I know why some readers tore into me for not including Radiohead in my previous book about depressing songs. I listened to "Creep" four times while doing my persnickety harmonic analysis and found myself getting more depressed each time. While it's supposedly about a wannabe stalker, "Creep" goes much deeper than that, exploring the insecurity and loneliness of the socially rejected. Thom Yorke plays the misfit loner who's smitten with a girl he's too scared to approach. "Couldn't look you in the eye," he moans as the progression plays behind him. She's an angel with skin that makes him cry. He sees her as a feather that floats in a beautiful world. He finishes the stanza with a heart-wrenching line that will be repeated throughout the song: "I wish I was special."

Yeesh. Draw the shades already. This is the saddest song to make the charts since REM's "Everybody Hurts." But before we can completely crawl under the covers, guitarist Jonny Greenwood slams out distorted stabs on his axe and a wall of crunch knocks us into the chorus. "I'm a creep," Yorke wails, a "weirdo." He's followed the girl to someplace he'd never be invited to and wonders what he's doing there. "I don't belong here," he says.

The band drops back down as Yorke wishes for a complete reality overhaul. He wants a perfect body, perfect soul, to have control over her life so that she'll notice him even when he's not around. He repeats his wish to be special, so special that his MySpace site will have more than three friends on it (yes, I know this song predates MySpace by more than a decade. Call the Anachronism Police). *CRUNCH. CRUNCH.* Greenwood's atonal thunderclaps appear again (how does he do that anyway?) and Yorke's chorus of sorrow is repeated. He's still a creep and a weirdo. In other words, he's like the rest of us who couldn't get plastic surgery when we were seventeen.

The girl must've noticed her infatuated pursuer because she

makes an embarrassed break for it. She runs out of the door as Yorke plaintively sings in a preternatural soprano: "She run, run . . ." Sadly enough, he's not surprised at her disdain for him. He understands, he only wants what makes her happy. Meanwhile, dozens of scornful eyes glare at him, mocking his presence among their social circle. The song ends with Yorke questioning his very existence among the living. "I don't belong here."

WHY IT'S CREEPY

Besides being extremely sad, "Creep" is unsettling because of the ugly truth in its lyrics while being anthemic all the same. There are any number of lonely teenagers, both male and female, who listen to "Creep" because it perfectly captures their inner turmoil of feeling rejected, isolated, and scorned by their peers. Adolescence is the new Sodom and Gomorrah, except that the meek are the ones being turned into salt pillars. God's wrath doesn't come with locusts and plagues anymore. He exacts His revenge on mankind by allowing rich teenage celebri-dicks to rule the zeitgeist (see Kevin Federline's "Lose Control"), while humility is scorned and originality condemned. This is the anxiety that "Creep" addresses so vividly. It doesn't encourage self-loathing, but rather mirrors it in a way that's powerful without being melodramatic. That is the essence of a song that connects with listeners and for that reason alone, "Creep" deserves more attention beyond its supposed connection to the Hollies.

Today, the rejected teenager of "Creep" is exposed to even more social tortures and peer ridicule than ever before. Acceptance is only accomplished if you can get on a reality show (when did teenage peer pressure get so bad that you have to please a fucking cable network?). Heed my words: salvation will come only after the rich white Orange County kids who star in those dumb-ass MTV reality shows are eaten by the sharks swimming offshore from their parents' beach houses.

The only taint there is to "Creep" is Radiohead's testy behavior towards concert fans wanting to hear the song that made them famous. They seem oddly ashamed of it, as if writing a hit is an aesthetic felony (only writing a bad one is). While I understand the weariness that comes with playing the same songs over and over again, it doesn't excuse chastising audience members who request it. "Creep" is still Radiohead's biggest-selling song and it's a great one to boot. So relax and sing it already. If the Rolling Stones can still do "Satisfaction," you can do "Creep."

STAN

Words and music by Eminen, Florian "Dido" Armstrong,
and Paul Herman
Performed by Eminem
Released 2000 (No. 52 in U.S., No. 1 in UK)

I ALREADY know I'm setting myself up for reader backlash by choosing to analyze Eminem's "Stan." People who love Eminem will be furious. People who dislike him will be bored. I'd skip it if I could but I can't. Like it or not, it's one of the creepiest songs of the last fifty years.

Most of you are probably familiar with "Stan," about the crazed Eminem fan who writes him letters and thinks his raps are serious. Supposedly it addresses critics who accuse Eminem of being a misogynist and homophobe. These critics, he insists, take his literal rap songs too literally and to illustrate, he wrote "Stan," yet another literal rap song. Eminem even got Elton John to perform it with him on the 2001 Grammy Awards (and was it just me or did Sir Elton kinda suck?).

"Stan" is from Eminen's multiplatinum *The Marshall Mathers Album*, which is deemed his masterpiece. I've listened to it. He says "bitch" a lot. He bashes on Britney and calls boy bands faggots. He slits his wife's throat in "Kim." Hey, whatever spins your turntable. Who am I to judge? I have no cultural ties to rap. I'm from Wisconsin; my heritage is beer and fat guys with accordions. I'm fine with Eminem being the biggest-selling rapper of all time. I'm fine that "Stan" has been called a cultural milestone by whoever is in charge of laying stones every cultural mile. I'm fine that rambling over a Dido single is considered the hip-hop equivalent of *Citizen Kane*. I'm fine with some critics declaring "Stan" the greatest rap song ever. I'm fine that fans of

Tupac or Biggie Smalls take umbrage at Eminem's status. Feel free to slug it out. I'll sell refreshments.

(OK, I've come this far without saying anything negative about Eminem directly. I wonder how long I can keep this up . . .)

THE SONG

"Stan" opens with thunder and rain sounds while Dido's "Thank You" is heard playing on a radio. She sings how she's having a lousy morning because her tea is cold, it's gloomy outside, one of her songs is on the radio, etc. The only thing that keeps her going is seeing someone's picture on the wall that she likes. As the music continues, we hear the sound of somebody else scratching out a handwritten letter. The person is writing to his rap idol "Slim" (Eminem) in the agitated style of someone who's either slightly unhinged or has been listening to Dido too much.

This would be Stan, who's such an Eminem fan he sounds exactly like Eminem.

Stan wonders why "Slim" hasn't answered his previous letters or called, even though he added his mobile, pager, and home phone numbers. He asks about Slim's daughter and mentions that his own girlfriend is pregnant. Stan offers condolences to Slim regarding the latter's "Uncle Ronnie," who apparently killed himself after a girlfriend rejected him.* Finally, Stan reminds "Slim" that he's his biggest fan and has all his CDs, posters, and even old underground recordings. All he asks for is a reply. He signs off, "Truly yours."

(Hmm, that wasn't so bad. I got this far without saying anything about the numbing sameness of Eminem's tracks, how his shut-up-bitch posturing and gunplay bullshit is a tired attempt at "keepin' it real," and that he largely appeals to upper-middle-class white kids who like the fact that he's white, too, because they can live vicariously through his tediously fraudulent rap narratives and not have to face the fact that their moms drive minivans . . .)

Yay, Dido's playing again, the same verse, too. Her tea's still cold and it's still raining. Freaky Stan is writing another letter and

---

* Eminem's real-life uncle Ron Polkingharn, only two months older than his nephew, committed suicide in 1990 at the age of nineteen.

he's pretty annoyed. He still hasn't heard from Slim and thinks it's "fucked up" that he doesn't reply to fan letters. What's worse is that Stan took his little brother Matthew to a concert and waited outside afterwards in the rain for an autograph. Slim just whisked by them without even looking. Bastard. Stan starts sharing a bit too much now, saying how he and Slim are just like each other; neither one knew their father. Stan's such a fan of Slim that he even had his idol's name tattooed on his chest. Ew, now he's writing how he cuts himself to see "how much it bleeds." He digs the pain. Stan signs off again, urging Slim to call him while adding a P.S. "We should be together."

(Phew. That was a lot of narrative. But I think I summarized it pretty accurately while staying objective. There's no need to mention those stupid "feuds" Eminem creates for publicity, like the one with Moby that made absolutely no sense. The confrontation with Triumph the Insult Comic Dog at the MTV Music Awards, when Eminem had to bring his idiot posse along to confront a sock puppet, I'll just skip that. I certainly won't suggest that a guy whose rap technique isn't any better than that of a dozen others gets all the accolades simply because he was the first Anglo to do the inner-city-rapper bit even though his whole act is about ten years behind the times . . .)

Um, Dido's still playing. We get to enjoy the first stanza over and over again (who was in charge of licensing?). Now Stan has gone crazy, throwing his expectant girlfriend in the trunk of his car and speeding off in a haze of vodka. He records his final message to Slim on a cassette recorder, about how betrayed he feels, how everybody lies, how he's mystified he actually owns a cassette recorder. Stan makes a mention of the old urban myth about a real-life drowning in Phil Collins's "In the Air Tonight." The girlfriend is screaming in the trunk as he speeds towards a bridge. The last thing we hear is Stan wondering how he can send the tape out. The car flies off the bridge, crashes into the water and kills them both.

(Now would be a good time to end this song. One more open

letter over a Dido accompaniment is enough to send me over a bridge, too.)

After another Dido interlude, Slim is heard writing back to Stan, apologizing for not answering sooner. He also scolds him about writing such crazy stuff and suggests he gets counseling. Slim says Stan should treat his girlfriend better and that he should stop hurting himself. The last thing he wants is for Stan to do some "crazy shit," like the guy he saw on the news who got drunk and drove his car off a bridge with his pregnant girlfriend in the trunk. They found a tape inside the car. The driver's name was . . . "it was you . . . damn!"

WHY IT'S CREEPY

In its own way, "Stan" is a love song: Slim is the object of Stan's warped, doomed affection. It's so direct in its storytelling that even your dog can comprehend it. That said, I'm not really sure where the cultural milestone stuff comes into "Stan." If we set aside all the knee-jerk Freudian interpretations and breathless psychoanalysis, we can see the song for what it is: Eminem talks while a Dido record plays behind him. When this approach to songwriting became "cutting edge" and "revolutionary," I'm not sure, but it's enough to creep me out. Maybe I'm biased or hanker too much for a predigital time in music that's gone forever. Perhaps the success of songs like "Stan" only confirms what I've long suspected, that rock 'n' roll is dead and younger groups like the Arctic Monkeys and Kaiser Chiefs are deluded in thinking they're carrying the torch. Today, producers win Grammys for turning on a drum machine and looping in prerecorded samples. Eminem garners international kudos for rapping pretty much the same thing over and over again. Fans who buy his CDs actually think he *composed* the tracks on his songs—but everything is created using other people's sampled tracks, few or no instruments, and a complete absence of any original music.

But as I said, I'm fine with it. Really, I am.

TOUCH ME, I'M SICK

THANK HEAVEN
FOR LITTLE GIRLS

Words by Alan Jay Lerner, music by Frederick Loewe
Performed by Maurice Chevalier
Released 1958 (no chart position)

IT'S LONG been socially acceptable for older men to hook up with younger women. Witness Michael Douglas with Catherine Zeta-Jones, Woody Allen with Soon Yi, Paul Simon with Edie Brickell, Harrison Ford with Calista Flockhart, etc. I'm guessing these women met them through a carbon-dating service.

On the other hand the opposite scenario is tainted with Oedipal baggage and Mrs. Robinson jokes. While I can't correct this double standard, I can at least confront the queasy song "Thank Heaven for Little Girls." Besides being a near-anthem for wrinkly guys drooling over nubile females, I've also learned that this creepy song is occasionally sung at receptions as a gift to the bride from her father. What new bridegroom wouldn't want to experience that at his wedding?

"Thank Heaven for Little Girls" originally appeared in the 1958 MGM musical *Gigi*, based on the 1945 novel by the French writer Colette. The novel *Gigi* is about a French girl being groomed to be a courtesan, a fancy word for a hooker who has tenure. Directed by Vincente Minelli (father of nutty Liza), *Gigi* disguised the cynical novel's setting with enough euphemisms and *My Fair Lady* froth to enable it to win ten Oscars, including Best Picture and Best Director. The film tells of a wealthy French playboy named Gaston who finds himself drawn to the peasant granddaughter of a family friend, the precocious Gigi. Gaston eventually learns of Gigi's courtesan training and that he's likely to become her first client. Realizing he's in love with Gigi, Gaston marries her instead. *Fin.*

One of *Gigi*'s showpiece musical numbers is "Thank Heaven for Little Girls," which Gaston's elderly uncle Honore sings in celebration of, well, little girls. While the song has been covered dozens of times by other artists, the original version from the film is what creeps out listeners the most. Legendary French entertainer Maurice Chevalier played Uncle Honore in the film and performed the song using a theeck French ack-SAANT that audiences of the time found charming. Today, he sounds like a lecherous professor at the Sorbonne.

THE SONG

The most effective way to creep yourself out with "Thank Heaven for Little Girls" is to imagine you're in a park where a large group of laughing preschool girls are playing nearby. Suddenly you look over and see a seventy-year-old guy sporting a top hat, white gloves, and a cane sitting in the middle of the kids' play area while leering around him. Before you call security, note that this is *the actual setting* where Uncle Honore sings the song in *Gigi*. This is all part of the magic of Hollywood, where otherwise deviant behavior is depicted as completely innocent. But while the film's audience is safely ensconced in its seats, you're literally in the park with this freaking old frog as he surveys the nymph pod around him. Honore notes how every time he sees a little girl or better yet, "five or six or seven," he can't avoid a "joyous urge" to exclaim, "Thaank Heavunn forr leeetle gairrls!" As you look on with mute horror, he adds that all little girls get "beeg-ger" every day, growing up in the most dee-laat-ful waay. All you can do is light up a cigarette, slug back some wine and think, *Who ees zis wee-ird guy? And where ees zat music coming frommm?* (Sorry, you're French, too.)

The next verse really knocks you for a loop. The old guy is singing about how little girls' eyes are so helpless and appealing (that would be an appeal for help, by the way). Ahh, but one day their little eyes will flash, he adds, and you'll be sent craashing thru ze ceei-ling, most likely with the vice squad following in hot pursuit. "Thaank Hea-vunn forr leeetle gairls," he repeats because without them, what would "leet-tle boys do?"

There's an orchestral interlude as leet-tle gairls flit around him while he beams like a lighthouse on amyl nitrate. You look on, nibbling on your Brie while muttering, "Sacré bleu! Zees ees geeting too straange pour moi. Where are ze par-raants?" Uncle Honore repeats his thanks to Heaven and you take off your beret, fill it up with rocks and throw it at him. "Take zat, you see-ck pear-vert!" Someone behind you yells "Cut!" and you turn to see a film crew glaring at you. They're American, so you already hate them.

WHY IT'S CREEPY

For any Maurice Chevalier fans I may have offended, please note that I'm quite aware that "Thank Heaven for Little Girls" is meant as a celebration of young girls who grow up to become ladies (also note that I'm mystified that you've actually heard of Maurice Chevalier). But *Gigi* was released in 1958, when the public was only afraid of nuclear attack, communism, and Jerry Lee Lewis. Little kids were left unsupervised because parents figured they'd be safe. If an old man wandered on to the playground and started singing the praises of leet-tle gairls, it was assumed that he was probably someone's dotty grandfather. Today, he'd have a bracelet attached to his ankle beeping like crazy.

Of all the old film genres, the classic movie musicals hold up the least. Their corny plots, silly dialogue, preternatural lighting, saturated colors, and ubiquitous songs give them a time-capsule veneer that leaves them looking dated. *Gigi* is a frothy confection that, while entirely watchable, looks slightly odd today when you consider it's about a young girl learning to become a kept woman on twenty-four-hour service call. If it's any consolation, *Gigi* isn't remotely as irritating as *Pretty Woman*. I've driven home nights on Santa Monica Boulevard enough times to know hookers look nothing like Julia Roberts.

YOU'RE BEAUTIFUL

Words and music by James Blunt
Performed by James Blunt
Released 2005 (No. 1 in U.S., No. 1 in UK)

LET'S GET one thing out of the way about "You're Beautiful."
Everybody hates this song. By everybody, I mean every human,
invertebrate, arthropod, marsupial, and creature that can fly or
swim. Leaves hate it. Statues hate it. Bricks hate it. Air hates it.
Even God hates it. The only person who doesn't hate "You're
Beautiful" is James Blunt. Give him time.

Wait a minute, I forgot someone. *I* don't hate "You're
Beautiful." I don't like it but I don't hate it either. ("Goodbye My
Lover," on the other hand, I loathe with every fiber of my being
and my cat's being.) It's more like I'm indifferent to "You're
Beautiful" because the song's about nothing. A guy sees a pretty
girl in the subway, notices that she's with some guy, and figures
he'll never be with her. That's the whole thing. It's a three-and-a-
half-minute song about an encounter that probably lasted ten
seconds. I'd leave "You're Beautiful" off the list except that I
already know I'll get ripped to shreds like I did when I left the
Smiths out of the depressing songs book. So for peace of mind,
I'm acquiescing to public opinion and including "You're
Beautiful." I admit that it's a little creepy, but I'm not sure that it
warrants a thousand words. As I said, nothing happens in this
song. But I'll try.

THE SONG

It's now three hours later.

I ran some errands, watered the plants, and figured out the
chords to a Nickleback song to see if there's a way to play it so

that it doesn't suck. I'm still stuck. Let's see, I could start with the intro. A strumming acoustic guitar plays some basic chords. Another acoustic plays a few notes. OK, that's done. I'll be right back—I have to turn on the sprinklers.

I'm back. Where was I? Let's see, he's waiting in the subway for the train to arrive when he sees an attractive girl. She smiles at him. He smiles back. This makes him think that his "life is brilliant" and he's just seen "an angel." He also sees that she's with another man, but no worries, he's got a plan. OK, that's done. I gotta turn off the sprinklers.

Back again. We're at the chorus. "You're beautiful," he sings. He sings it again. And again. But he doesn't know what to do and figures he'll never be with her. I guess he doesn't have a plan. That's done. Off to the bar.

Back again. What a great happy hour. I put away five, six beers. I'm smashed. What song am I on again? Oh, yeah, "You're Fucking Beautiful." I thought it was over. Didn't he just say he'll never see her again? Oh, for chrissakes, now he's recapping how he first saw her. Apparently she caught his eye when they passed each other. She could tell he was stoned. He'll never see her again, but at least they had "a moment." OK, that's done. I gotta take a wicked piss.

I'm back. It's the chorus again. He sings it again. And again. We hear about how he saw her in the crowd. Again. We hear how he'll never be with her. Again. He sings "You're beautiful." Again. And again. Finally, he thinks that somewhere there's another angel, who arranged for him to be with the girl he saw. Instead we hear he'll never be with her. Again. OK, that's done. I gotta take another piss.

WHY IT'S CREEPY

Sorry when I drink this much I tend to type expository verse in long run-on sentences with no full stops or commas in between but it's obvious that a song like "You're Beautiful" doesn't have anywhere near enough content to warrant a comprehensive analysis and that the only reason I'm including it at all is because everybody in the galaxy hates this song and thinks its creepy and thinks it deserves to be royally eviscerated in print because the song was overplayed so much on the radio and everyone got sick of it though it still became a number-one hit and has gone on to be one of the most requested songs at weddings which if you think about it makes absolutely no sense because it's about a guy who's too stoned to approach a girl he saw for a few seconds on a subway platform and so he just repeats over and over how beautiful she is but won't ever see hear again anyway which is completely the wrong message to have expressed at a wedding and you'd have to be a fucking retard to request that it be played at your wedding since all the guests who hate the song anyway will hear the lyrics again and wonder why the bride and groom are so dense that they think it's a good idea to play it before they take their vows.

OK, that's done. I'm gonna go to bed.

By the way, *now* I hate this song.

PIECES OF ME

Words and music by Ashlee Simpson, Kara DioGuardi, and
John Shanks
Performed by Ashlee Simpson
Released 2004 (No. 5 in U.S., No. 4 in UK)

I'M NOT making any comments about Ashlee Simpson's lip-synching fiasco on the NBC show *Saturday Night Live*. That'd be hypocritical because honestly, after working long hours I get so exhausted from typing that I'm unable to write live. That's when I resort to type-synching. I pretend to type while a prewritten document is typed out for me. In fact, I'm doing it right now. The words you're reading were actually typed in advance; I'm just miming along. If done correctly, the reader MY CLOCK ISN'T A SHERPA can't tell the difference. Because of fatigue I've chosen to type-sync this chapter on the Ashlee Simpson hit "Pieces of Me" GORILLA BUYS DONUTS rather than write it normally LY LY LY LY LY LY LY LY LY.

In 2004, Ashlee Simpson was the guest musical act on *Saturday Night Live* and was about to POODLE EXPLODES perform her song "Autobiography" when her prerecorded voice was heard singing "Pieces of Me," which she'd already performed earlier on the show. Mortified, she slunk off the stage and into YouTube infamy. She later claimed she suffered from acid reflux and needed a backing track, but that her drummer pushed the wrong button (as drummers are wont to do). While she's still the butt of jokes because of it, I've chosen not to pile on. Besides, "Pieces of Me" is plenty creepy even without the stigma of performance fraud hanging over it OVER HANGING FRAUD PERFORMANCE OF STIGMA.

THE SONG

"Pieces of Me" begins with Edie Brickell and the New Bohemians standing outside the studio asking for their music back. OK, I'm kidding, but "Pieces of Me" features the same loping syncopated guitar figure and white man's jazz-folk groove that infects half of their CDs. After eight bars, Ashlee, stressed and harried, recounts her busy busy week. On Monday she's "waiting," while on Tuesday she's "fading." No wonder she's exhausted. Still, by Wednesday she can't sleep. Fortunately the phone rings for her and it's the love of her life ~~Josh Ryan Wilmer Chris Braxton Pete Taye~~ INSERT NAME HERE who has come to rescue her from the IF 2X IS THE COSINE OF PI darkness. His arrival makes Ashlee fall, indeed "fall so fast." It's so exhilarating that she can hardly "catch my breath."

I know what you're thinking: what's so creepy about this? She's singing about missing her boyfriend. Where's the clingy declaration, the bitter jealousy, the exhumed corpse? All valid points WEINER DOGGY WEINER DOG but hold on, there's the chorus. It's all fine and innocent at first, she's resting her head on him, she likes how it feels, etc., but then she sings how he can tell "all the pieces, pieces, pieces of me." It's at this point that I'm realizing there are pieces of Ashlee Simpson strewn around the room. Even worse, he can seemingly identify each piece. "Bicep . . . femur . . . lymph gland . . . liver . . . parietal lobe . . ."

The next stanza finds a reassembled Ashlee admitting she can be "moody" and "restless" but good ole what's-his-name doesn't let it bother him. Instead, he listens when she's angry while making sure she's happy again; "It's your mission." She proceeds to rest her head on him and then, WHAP! She's in pieces all over again. "Patella . . . trapezius . . . spleen . . . clavicle . . ."

An inconsequential bridge that barely spans a storm drain reveals how he knows everything she's about to say. I should hope so since it's probably prerecorded (sorry, couldn't resist). REMOVE STEAK AND BLESS THE SHOE POLISH. Ashlee then repeats her weekly schedule, still "waiting" on Monday while "fading into his axe-wielding arms" on Tuesday. The song concludes with the anatomical mantra "Pieces, pieces, pieces of me . . ." only to be repeated when her drummer hits the wrong button (sorry again).

WHY IT'S CREEPY

"Pieces of Me" may be the only creepy love song where the title is everything. It's not a terrible song. I've heard a thousand singles much worse, and its Brickell/Bohemians lilt is somewhat infectious. The thing that disturbs me is the "pieces" reference HARRY POTTER IS THE ANTICHRIST. When you watch any videos of her "performing" the song, it's very creepy to see her mooning over some guy who can tell all the pieces of her. The first time I heard it I thought, who's this *Texas Chainsaw* fan singing this song? Yes, I know it means all the pieces of her personality, her feelings, her soul, whatever, but even that's problematic. Ashlee is either deluded, too deferent, or dating Leatherface.

While it's unlikely Ashlee Simpson would have a record contract if her last name were Kuwalski, she isn't a horrible singer, just not a great one (though her booed performance at the Orange Bowl half-time show was embarrassing) BORON ATOMS MAKE FLOORS LOOK LIKE SINGER FROM BLUR. But if you track the number of televised performances she's done where she's clearly lip-synching, it's clear that her representatives are more interested in marketing a surname than showcasing an artist. Unfortunately, they're making a lot of money doing it so who can blame them? No wonder everyone wants pieces of her.

~~N~~A~~U~~G~~H~~T~~Y ~~GIRL~~ D~~I~~RR~~T~~Y

Christina Aguilera, Dana Stinson, Reggie Noble,
Words and music by ~~Beyoncé Knowles, Scott Storch,~~
~~Robert Waller, Angela Beyince,~~
Jasper Cameron, and Balewa Muhammed
~~Donna Summer, Peter Belotte, and Giorgio Moroder~~
Performed by ~~Beyoncé~~ Christina Aguilera
Released ~~2004 (No. 3 in U.S., No. 10 in UK)~~ 2002
(No. 48 in U.S., No. 1 in UK)

ATTENTION, EVERYONE. ~~Beyoncé~~ Christina Aguilera wants
to bang you. Yes, that ~~luscious R&B~~ miniature pop singer ~~with~~
~~the moniker made from leftover Scrabble letters~~ who's another
seedy alumnus of the Mickey Mouse Club will do anything
to get into the sack with you and your friends. She's calling all her
girls to come along. She saw you checking her out in the club,
when you looked over and thought, Why's she dressed like a
whore? ~~Beyoncé~~ Christina is wasting no time with any of that
boring conversation stuff or a test for STDs. Let's get it on, let's
do it, let's head on over to ~~Beyoncé's~~ Christina's place and get
naaaaaasty.

Sorry for the confusion. I'm still narrowing down my skank
songs. This chapter was even more disorganized yesterday
because I was also considering Britney Spears, Shakira, Nelly
Furtado, Pink, Mya, L'il Kim, Lindsay Lohan, and whoever those
Rocky Horror tramps were that butchered "Lady Marmalade" a
few years back (What? Oh. Never mind). I've lost count of how
many times I've seen these girls do the Spin-and-Splay in their
videos, where they spin around and then splay themselves against
a wall. That move is more tired than a stint in rehab. As for the
songs (you known the ones I'm talking about), they're always a

digital clump of blooping burping loops and samples underpinning a lot of come-and-shag-me lyrics. Throw in a stripper-themed video and *voila*, you have pop music's latest invention, the slut operetta.

While the competition is ongoing, I'm throwing in the towel and going with Christina Aguilera's "Dirrty." The extra "r" is supposed to make the song sound dirtier. In that case, add an extra "t" to shitty and we're covered.

THE SONG

When a song has more cowriters listed than musicians playing on it, I already know it's going to be one of those dance pop/rap hybrid tracks that gets auto-assembled a dozen times a day on a Korg Workstation. Five would-be geniuses collaborated on "Dirrty," including rapper Redman, the result being an appalling number of verses that say everything while saying nothing. It's a lot of "gonna" this, "wanna" that, which makes analyzing it like dissecting a tree branch. Don't be surprised if I get bored and watch the music video instead.

"Dirrty" opens with Redman gracing us with his Keats- and Byron-inspired rap poetry. "Dirrty. Filthy. Nasty. You nasty." From here, a house beat enters monotonously while a bass heavy Sly Stone–like riff leaves digital skid marks on the track. After aimless chanting about ringing the alarm and "throwin' elbows," Christina finally shows up, grunting short elliptical phrases that never complete a thought, how she's "overdue," needs some "room," paid her "dues," is in the "mood," the kind of near-rhymes you get from lyricists who think a thesaurus is a creature out of *Jurassic Park*. Anyway, Christina's corralled her girls so they can start getting "dirrty" because it's what she needs to get off. She's gonna sweat till she strips naked. OK, over to the video.

Well, there's Christina wearing some sort of panties-and-chaps ensemble from Victoria's Secret Cowpunching Collection. She's in a boxing ring with her backup dancers surrounded by hundreds of hip-hot heathens doing the sycophantic extras shuffle. More pronoun-deficient lines about jumping, dancing on tables, throwing glasses, while she whips-snaps-writhes-gyrates about like a lap dancer entertaining all of Luxembourg. The "gonna" phrases come fast and furious, as she gets the girls, gets the boys, makes some noise. She "wanna get dirrty."

The decadence turns redundant as everyone packs around Christina while sweat is dripping down her body. But the lyrics start sounding all Madison Avenue minimalist now— "Drop your cups, give all you got, get it rough"—the kind of dopey directives you see in a Nike ad. It probably doesn't matter because Ms. Aguilera has changed to a short short miniskirt and bikini top, exposing more of her flaxen skin to the dirrty proceedings around her. She's boxing with some female venereal carrier as shirtless members of Redman's posse officiate without a rulebook. It's such a turn-on, she says it's time they take it "to the parking lot" and hump until someone "calls the cops."

I'm turning off the video now because Redman just arrived with one of those why-is-this-here rap interludes that infects way too many pop tracks nowadays. This bling-wearing idiot pulls every tired cliche out of da hood handbag, spitting about his car, his gear, his dead presidents, while using "pimp" as a verb. The remainder of it is solipsistic slang that adds up to minus four in total weight while meaning absolutely nothing. He ends it by barking.

God, this song is still going on. You could count the number of notes in the melody on Hitler's testicles. Christina's soaking wet now from writhing on a waterlogged floor. Between her and her girls, I've seen more doggie positions assumed than at a breeder's kennel. She's still looking for someone to get her off and there's a shot of her clamping her legs around the waist of a shirtless male extra. "Wanna get dirrty . . ."

WHY IT'S CREEPY

While the music video for "Dirrty" looks like Caligula's senior prom, even without it the song feels like a compendium of cheesy pick-up lines being yelled over a booming sound system. The lascivious phrases eventually sound tired, while Redman's rap is useless. Look, I like an erotically charged song from time to time (see "I Touch Myself"), but what makes the slut operettas like "Dirrty" so bad-creepy is the disingenuous bullshit that comes with them, where women singers insist that rubbing their labias against a fire pole demonstrates "female empowerment." Please. Just say, "Look, guys think I'm hot, so I'm doing this to help sell albums." Christina has some of the best pipes in the business, but her power-through-pelvic-thrust rationale doesn't cut it here.

Not a few of the aforementioned contemporaries of Christina have played up the empowerment paradox, as in Beyoncé's "Naughty Girl," in which she becomes "empowered" by picking up a stranger at a club and allowing him to ravage her and her invited girlfriends. Lindsay Lohan spends most of her video screen time for her single "Rumors" performing Spin-and-Splay in a club while making out in a back room with a guy she's known for thirteen seconds. Nelly Furtado boasts about being "promiscuous." Don't even get me started with Britney.

MAKING LOVE OUT
OF NOTHING AT ALL

Words and music by Jim Steinman
Performed by Air Supply
Released 1983 (No. 2 in U.S., No. 80 in UK)

I REALLY wanted to get through this book without having to deal with Air Supply. Everything about the Aussie duo of Russell Hitchcock and Graham Russell hearkens back to the oxygen deprivation implied in their moniker. Who can sit through "All Out of Love" without feeling lightheaded? Who can withstand "Every Woman in the World" without seeing spots? Who can endure "The One That You Love" without collapsing unconscious while brain damage slowly sets in? Who in the hell bought these guys' records?

Turns out we Americans did. Air Supply were more popular in the U.S. than in their native Australia (so that's why Europeans think Americans are stupid). They scored eight Top-10 singles in the U.S. alone from 1980 to 1983, yet everyone claimed they hated them. Granted my crew was bonging up to REO Speedwagon, so they weren't exactly harbingers of taste either but, seriously, what alien conspiracy was behind all this Airhead popularity? They seemingly released the same sappy ballad over and over again while always featuring Hitchcock's thrown-off-a-bridge tenor.

So now, not only am I contending with a creepy Air Supply song, but also it happens to be one written by Jim Steinman, the hirsute Wagner of pop music. Mr. Steinman is the songwriter behind Meat Loaf's *Bat Out of Hell* album and the notorious Bonnie Tyler song "Total Eclipse of the Heart," which I include in my depressing songs book. He writes every song as if it were the last act of the opera and the vengeful ghost is laying waste to the proscenium. I almost feel bad (I said almost) that I'm including yet another one of his nutso songs in this book, but then again, I didn't ask him to pair up with Air Supply.

THE SONG

One of Steinman's lyrical devices is to see how many different ways he can say the same thing repeatedly until it drives everyone crazy. After a tinkling piano intro, vocalist Hitchcock starts teeing up a series of phrases that he knocks down the fairway with rotelike ease. "I know just how to whisper," he sings, while adding that he also knows how to "cry." Wow, you know how to whisper *and* cry? What a gymnast you are. The thing is, we have to wait as Hitchcock lists everything else he can do. He knows just how to:

> find answers,
> lie,
> fake it,
> scheme,
> tell the truth,
> dream.

Right, then we— What? There's *more*? He knows just how to:

> touch,
> prove,
> pull someone closer,
> let them loose.

Fine, I got it. From here, the—Oh, you gotta be freaking kidding.

> *And I know . . .*
> *The night is fading*
> *Time is flying.*

OK, stop. We get it, you know how to do everything, except how to shut up and get to the point. What can't you do? "I don't know how to leave you," Hitchcock sings. He also doesn't know how she can make love "out of nothing at all."

Everything up to here is both textbook Air Supply and routine Jim Steinman, with Hitchcock's Doppler-effect tenor mole-whacking each one of Steinman's compulsive phrases with MOR precision. Meanwhile, neurotic piano and bad 1980s orchestration bury everything except the choir.

Finally, even Steinman has grown sick of the *and I know just* motive and changes up the music into a long, strange bridge. It's here that he employs his other favorite exasperating device, which is crammingasmanywordsashepossiblycaninto a single melodic phrase. Hitchcock sings how the sun's rays form a stream through her hair, except it's alotwordierthanthatbecause heforcessomanywordstogether. There are some generic references to a heart beating like a drum, some stars aiming like spotlights, basically a lot of greeting card imagery that's been around since Pompeii was leveled. There's even a beacon that forever brightens the darkness. (Correction, imagery that's been around since Pompeii was being built.)

After a banal guitar solo, Hitchcock is back to his list again, this time about sports. Now he can make runners stumble, he can make every tackle, he can even make "all the stadiums rock." (Um, this is Air Supply we're talking about here, right?) My favorite accomplishment is when he says he can make the night "disappear by the dawn." How'd he pull that one off? Still, he'll never make it without her and he's never going to make it like she does "Making Love Out of Nothing at All . . ."

WHY IT'S CREEPY

Meat Loaf could've easily wrapped his beefy pipes around "Making Love" as it has all the cadences that Mr. Bat Out of Hell is known for. Alas, it was Air Supply who served it to us, and no one is the better off for it. I'm amazed this song nearly hit No. 1 and cannot understand why nobody went postal from the egregious lyrical repetition and chain-reaction verses in the song's middle section. While I've been accused of choosing inappropriate songs just so that I can bash them, I can make a solid case as to why "Making Love Out of Nothing at All" is so damned creepy. It's because the lyrics make anyone who sings it sound like an insufferable egomaniac who cannot understand why his girl left him. When his accomplishments include crying, whispering, and scheming, you wonder if his resume resembles a novella. This song is the anthem of the first generation of New Age sensitive-men types who appeared on talk shows in the early eighties talking about their favorite Alan Alda movies. They boasted about their sensitivity to women's needs and ridiculed the macho types who they felt gave men a bad name. But underneath all their feminist empathy and altruistic gestures they were a bunch of pompous, egoistic jerks who honestly thought the moon was theirs to give the women in their lives. It was a phase that didn't last long, because women got sick of them and went to find guys with Harleys. As for the sensitive men, they're probably the bastards who bought all those Air Supply records. That might explain it.

AFTERNOON DELIGHT

Words and music by Bill Danoff
Performed by the Starland Vocal Band
Released 1976 (No. 1 in U.S., No. 18 in UK)

MOST ONE-HIT wonders don't get any respect. Personally I love them as long as they did a great song; Big Country's "In a Big Country" still rocks my socks. Plus, one-hit wonders are convenient. I can enjoy one song by someone without committing myself to their entire music career. It's just like sex in college. But the ugly flipside is something like "Afternoon Delight," which inexplicably bulleted the charts only to become the most despised thing ever. I also have my own traumatic experience with this song (more on that later).

A few readers of my last book criticized me for selecting songs they'd never heard of. Well, if you've never heard of "Afternoon Delight," please tell me who designed the bomb shelter you live in so they can build me one. While the group behind it has long vanished, the song continues to appear in movies and TV shows for the purpose of ironic comedy. "Hey, let's play 'Afternoon Delight' during the scene when they're hunting elk!" Har-de-har-har.

A creepy ode to daylight boffing, "Afternoon Delight" was released in 1976 by the Starland Vocal Band, one of the lamest musical acts ever. How lame? One of their singers was named Taffy. Nobody should ever be named Taffy, be it a dog, hamster, rhesus monkey, piranha, or female vocalist of a pool-cue-up-the-ass painful seventies group. Still, Starland Vocal Band ended up being awarded two Grammies for "Afternoon Delight" and even hosted their own summer variety TV show.

THE SONG

When it came to the time for me to analyze "Afternoon Delight," I listened to it once. That was all I needed because the song is like a Matthew McConaughey movie: experience it once and you'll know how bad it is. After eight bars of folk-pop strumming, lead singer Bill Danoff sings about how he's "gonna find my baby, gonna hold her tight," revealing his poetic debt to my first-grade teacher who taught us how to read. His goal, you see, is to get himself some "afternoon delight" by banging his girl during the TV soaps. No need to wait until "the cold dark night," when you can see everything better in the light of day. The Opry harmonies of girl vocalists Taffy Nivert and Margot Chapman come in and sing how "thinkin' of you is workin' up my appetite" and they can't wait for their afternoon delight. There are two problems with this line. First, you work up *an* appetite, not *my* appetite. Second, one of the people singing is named Taffy.

While everything up to this point is creepy-crawly cutesy, the chorus is plain loony. "Sky rockets in flight," they sing, at which point a dive-bombing whooshing sound is heard, apparently to show us what an orgasm sounds like: napalm bombing from an F-14. A pedal steel guitar countrifies the proceedings even more while things take a graphic turn.

His day begun, Danoff sings in the next stanza, with him feeling so polite, adding how you can't catch a fish "that didn't bite." It's here that the metaphor goes south (if you know what I mean) as he tells his girl that she's got some "bait a-waiting" and now he's eager to start "nibbling a little afternoon delight." This may be the first time that coy cunnilingus ever appeared in a Top 40 song. Then back to the chorus (WHOOOOOOOSSSH).

Following an inconsequential bridge in which a rhyme is made from phrases "come around" and "goes down" (insert juvenile snickering here), the lines about appetites getting worked up while sticks and stones get rubbed together are repeated and we hear the Air Force climaxing chorus one last time. The song finishes with a pretentious cadenza of four-part harmonies in which everyone sings the "aft-" syllable of the word "afternoon" (take that, Crosby, Stills, and Nash!) until they finally finish.

WHY IT'S CREEPY

Double-entendre is a standard device in songwriting and, granted, the ones on display in "Afternoon Delight" are tame in today's world of Christina Aguilera's "Dirrty." But when you combine the group's sugary vocals and elementary school rhymes with their desire to gnaw each other's bait, well, that's really too much information, especially when one of the singers is named Taffy. With its Nashville harmonies and Laurel Canyon acoustic guitars, the song fiendishly combines the influence of music's two lamest creative conclaves. Like many gimmicky hit singles that wear out their welcomes ("Macarena," "Who Let the Dogs Out," etc.), "Afternoon Delight" terminally ruined the Starland Vocal Band and they broke up in 1980. Years later I saw one of those *Where Are They Now?* specials and learned that two of their members were working as estate agents. *C'est la vie.*

I have my own nightmarish true experience with "Afternoon Delight." While still in high school in Wisconsin, I played guitar in the jazz ensemble and spent a fair amount of time in the music department, where an ARP Axxe synthesizer was kept in a practice room. I would spend hours experimenting with it, dialing up all kinds of obnoxious sounds from its oscillators, including a replication of the whooshing sound in "Afternoon Delight" (no, I didn't have a life back then). Coincidentally, the school was staging its annual variety show and one of the songs being performed was "Afternoon Delight." My best friend Steve, an excellent musician, had agreed to play guitar and sing the lead vocal. Like me, he hated "Afternoon Delight," but the two girls singing the harmony parts were cute and they'd asked him so what the hell? For reasons I still can't recall, I was drafted into adding the song's whooshing orgasm sound on the synthesizer. I rehearsed with them a few times, which involved twiddling my thumbs until they got to "sky rockets in flight . . ." I hit the synth key, pulled a slider switch, and WHOOOSSHH!! Convinced I was Brian Eno, I waited for the big night where I could show off my prowess on an ARP keyboard.

The evening arrived and the auditorium was packed. I sat in the front row next to a pretty blonde girl in one of my classes, the synthesizer set up on the floor below the edge of the stage. We watched as students performed songs from *Oliver*, Dolly Parton, and the Statler Brothers. It was all wholesome and squeaky-clean, so I couldn't wait to get up there and blow sonic sexuality over the proceedings. Finally, Steve and his girls walked out on stage to applause. I got up, went over to the synth and sat down, waiting. The song began and they sang flawlessly. They hadn't gone eight bars when suddenly—

WHHOOOOOSSSSSSSSHHHHHHH!!!!!

A sound like a blizzard blown out of a walrus's sphincter came out of nowhere. Horrified, I looked at the synthesizer. It was prematurely ejaculating. I hadn't even touched it yet it was blasting away. I yanked off the volume. On stage, I could see the girls turning beet-red while Steve tried not to laugh. I cheated the volume back up and waited until they got to the chorus. Whooosh! I went, relieved that it worked correctly. Thinking everything was fine, I sat back. Steve and the girls sang about bait and nibbling each other—

WHHOOOOOSSSSSSSSHHHHHHH!!!!!

The cursed thing was jacking off again. Mouthing obscenities, I yanked down the volume. The director glared daggers at me while the audience wondered why this lunatic was shooting salvoes over their heads. Knowing I had one more cue to make, I eased the volume up again and prayed it would behave.

WHHOOOOOSSSSSSSSHHHHHHH!!!!!

It was hopeless. My electronic debut was being thwarted by a masturbating synthesizer. We managed to finish the song and I slunk back to my seat while the eyes of a hundred sets of parents shot lasers at me. The cute blonde girl looked at me and asked in dulcet tones, "What the hell was *that*?"

I never touched the ARP Axxe again.

YOUR BODY IS A WONDERLAND

Words and music by John Mayer
Performed by John Mayer
Released 2001 (No. 24 in U.S.)

THE GHOSTLY double of a living person is called a doppelganger, a heady word of German origin. Walk through a crowded shopping center and if you see someone who looks exactly like you, you've witnessed your doppelganger (or a complete stranger who resembles you, but what fun is that?). Traditionally, a doppelganger is a bad twin that manifests itself in order to take over the other person's life, which could explain Robert De Niro's movie career during the last ten years. It also helps to put the musical career of John Mayer in perspective, because as far as I'm concerned, there are two of them wandering around, a source and an evil Xerox. One makes girls swoon with his sensitive adult contemporary songwriter act; the other one has a jones for Stevie Ray Vaughan.

When Mayer first came upon the music scene in 2001, it was via his harmless but bland hit song "No Such Thing." It helped his major-label debut CD, *Room for Squares*, go platinum while giving foes of Dave Matthews one more singer to be annoyed with. Mayer was good-looking, preppy, young, and marketable. College girls found him adorable, their boyfriends thought him irritating. This would logically be the "good" John Mayer. Then audiences discovered another John Mayer, a wicked guitar player with a soulful voice who worshipped Johnny Winter, Buddy Guy, and other blues legends. This John Mayer formed a power trio, played R&B and Hendrix covers, opened for the Rolling Stones, and jammed with Eric Clapton. Again, logic dictates this to be the doppelganger, a sinister John Mayer bent on experimenting, taking risks, and screwing up an established pop music career.

Actually, the roles should be reversed. The "good" John Mayer is the one who skillfully wields a Strat while covering "Little Wing" in concert, while the doppelganger is the evil prick who wrote "Your Body Is a Wonderland."

THE SONG

"Your Body" begins with John popping syncopated chords against an Anglo beat while telling us he's got the afternoon off and his girl has a room for them. The only thing left is for her to "discover me discovering you," which if you think about it is exactly how a woman finds out some pervert is peering into her bathroom window. The inevitable analysis of her body comes next. It starts off fine if unoriginal, saying her skin is like porcelain. Then the first creepy moment in the song happens, when Mayer gleefully describes her as having "candy lips" and a "bubblegum tongue." When I try to visualize this, I see a woman's mouth stuck to the bottom of my shoe.

The setup for the chorus involves the happy couple swimming in a "deep sea of blankets" as they cancel all their plans for the day, including downloading the new John Mayer album and rotating the tires on the Volvo. He sighs how her body's a wonderland, a place where he'll lose his hands (I don't want to know where).

The next stanza commits the age-old error of utilizing awkward lyrics so as not to upset a rhyme. First he admires how her hair falls around her "face," but then he decides to rhyme it with "I love the shape you take when crawling towards the pillowcase." How does somebody change shape while crawling towards a pillowcase? Worse, he reassures her that he'll never let her head hit the bed without "my hand behind it." I'm completely at a loss as to what this means, other than maybe the girl is a pillow-chasing nut who likes to ram her skull into the headboard.

After more sea-of-blankets bullshit, they're off to discover her wonderland body again, losing his hands in the process. There's a tenuous bridge that involves him mumbling about feeling frustrated and that it hurts to see how good-looking she is (yeah, having a hot girlfriend is always agonizing). Following a pithy guitar solo, Mayer finishes up with further declarations of how her body's a wonderland while ad-libbing some da-da-dah vocalizing until the engineer gets bored and fades the track.

WHY IT'S CREEPY

If there's one word that sums up "Your Body Is a Wonderland," it's *precious*. This is a bad word because backwards it's pronounced "sick-urp." Anything that's precious in a song wears off in twenty-three seconds (I counted) and then it's a sticky ride downhill. There are way too many sick-urp elements to this song: the bobbing bass, the cutesy guitar figure, the timid drums, the I-just-woke-up-and-feel-horny vocal, the music video starring an embarrassed Mayer singing to a chick actor he obviously met that day. Everything in "Your Body" starts off precious and ends up sick-urp.

While it's clearly about Mayer spending a lazy day boffing his girlfriend, the way he describes it sucks out all the seduction and replaces it with a pimply kid with Asperger's Syndrome sneaking into a cheerleader's bedroom to cop a feel (I'm assuming she's wasted, otherwise she wouldn't be hitting her head all the time). The first time I heard "Your Body Is a Wonderland" with its candy lips and bubblegum tongue, my forehead knitted so much that it made a sweater. I don't care how rich and talented Mayer is, what girl in her right mind would service a guy who said her tongue was like bubble gum (would you want it touching your bare skin)? This cannot possibly be the same guy who took a year off to tour clubs with a blues rock band and trade licks with Buddy Guy. It's the evil doppelganger, I tell you, and he's the one with the record contract.

PRIDE AND JOY

Words and music by David Coverdale
Performed by Coverdale-Page
Released 1993 (No. 1 on U.S. Rock Tracks)

AS A serious scholar of rock music history, I've spent many hours doing research at the Rock 'n' Roll Hall of Archives, which is a pentagram-shaped building located in a field a few kilometers west of Stonehenge. The archives are only open at night, because the staff is too hungover during the day to work. The Rock 'n' Roll Hall of Archives houses the world's largest collection of letters, notes, memos, and drunken scribblings by rock music's biggest luminaries. While there researching what kind of microphone Axl Rose prefers to throw at audience members, I came across a series of typed letters sent to legendary guitarist Jimmy Page by a disgruntled former member of one of his bands. I've excerpted them below.

January 13, 1993
From the Desk of: Robert Plant
TO: Jimmy Page
RE: This bollocks called Coverdale-Page

Dear Mr. Page,

My name is Robert Plant and I'm a singer who's gigged in a few rock bands over the years. I got started with Band of Joy when I was just a wee lad of 17 and scuffled with them for a spell. Then I hooked up with this bloke who used to play with the Yardbirds and together we formed a group called Led Zeppelin. Maybe you've heard of them since YOU WERE IN THE BLEEDIN' BAND WITH ME, YOU TWAT!!

So I come in from feeding the swans, sit down for a spot of tea, and pick up the new copy of *NME* only to read that you're working with David bleedin' Coverdale. What, Ozzy was too busy? What is this shite? I cannot believe you'd partner up with that git who fronts Whitesnore, Wipe Snake, whatever they're called.

Here's what they wrote: "Former Led Zeppelin guitarist Jimmy Page has joined forces with Whitesnake's golden-maned vocalist David Coverdale to form The Coverdale-Page Project." Wow, a golden-maned vocalist? Musta been hard to find someone like that. How wasted were you from '68 to '80? I tolerated it when you worked with Paul Rodgers because he sings four bloody octaves lower than me. But Coverdale? Everyone knows he's a Robert Plant wannabe. He wears his shirts like I do, styles his hair like I do, interjects the word 'baby' 30 times in a song like I do. Did you see him at California Jam when he was with Deep Purple, and Blackmore went bat-shit and destroyed his equipment? Watch the footage. He even registers bewilderment like I do.

It says here you two are already working on an album together. Well, la dee da. Hope you've got your mandolin tuned up for the 'Goin' to California,' retread you're probably recording right now. Does the theremin still work?

I hope you two bleeding twits have a happy life together. Not! (I heard it in a flick once. I think it's funny.)

Robert

THE SONG

April 10, 1993
From the Desk of: Robert Plant
TO: Jimmy Page
RE: 'Pride and Joy,' creepy new single from Coverdale-Page album

Dear Judas,

Me again. Well, you did it. You and Cover-Plant, sorry, Coverdale released your little 'project' CD. I had my assistant get a copy from the Virgin store and I just listened to it. It sounds like the last two Zep albums played at half speed. I didn't know whether to have déjà vu or a seizure.

So that creepy 'Pride and Joy' is all over Laser 88 radio. Good God, man, a song about deflowering a bloody schoolgirl? Aren't you a little long in the fangs for that? You're gonna be 50 next year. You start the song off with that nervous strumming thing you always do while Coverdull is singing about some little chick taking him to the river, then to the sea, then asks her to '*pour your ocean over me.*' How many bodies of water does he need? Then he's telling her to scratch her name across his back. Lemme get this straight: He's lying on top of her while she's doing calligraphy below his shoulder blades? She must be bored out of her mind.

I was waiting for the 'Black Dog' guitar break you like to throw in and, sure enough, there it was after the intro. You got the drummer to play exactly like Bonzo did, too. I didn't mind that but when Crapperdale starts caterwauling, I almost want to get on the phone with my lawyers. Do you have any idea how much he *sounds* like me?! When he screams about the diamonds on her ankles and the sapphires on her shoes, he might as well be lip-synching to *Physical Graffiti*. I got all queasy hearing him call her 'Mama's little princess' and 'Daddy's pride and joy.' When he says he's like a kid playing with her 'toys,' I'm, like, bloody hell, he's using my shagging references from when I was 21.

Bollocks, now Clappertail's going on about her shakin' and wakin' him, how she's so wild that he's gonna name a hurricane after her. Let's name one after him, he's the one who blows. And did he just call her 'little miss dynamite' and 'youngblood'? We didn't even call our worst groupies that.

Ah, the instrumental break. It says on the liner notes that you're playing the harmonica. Since when did you start playing harmonica? Anyway, I got to sit through that.

Oh Lord, Cropperstool is repeating his river/sea/ocean demands again. Just drown the bugger already and tell the bird to scratch 'wrinkly old perv' across his back instead. I'm not buying his claim he'll sleep outside her door either. He should be sleeping under her crib.

At last it's over. It's short but you still managed to cram in half your licks, all of my vocals, and an underage girl with an uncanny ability at finding waterways. Cheers, mate, and tell Clovenhoof to stay the hell out of my octave.

WHY IT'S CREEPY

November 3, 1993
From the Desk of: Robert Plant
TO: Jimmy Page
RE: Unledded project

Dear Jimmy,

Well, well, look who comes crawling back. I read how you and Cravendick decided to shelve the 'Project' and cancel your tour because you two couldn't fill an eel pie shop in Brighton. Now you want us to reunite and do old Zep songs with hurdy gurdys and Moroccan banjos. I told you that single 'Pride and Joy' was great. *Not!* (I still think that's funny.) You just can't keep doing songs about shagging teen girls at our age. When Cloppercloop brought the bloody tune in, why didn't you look him in the eye and say, 'Mate, I'm 50. You're 41. Robert and me wrote this stuff when we were in our early 20s.' Mind you, I never woulda wrote 'little miss dynamite' even when I was bleeding 13 years old. So now you're stuck with a bunch of unreleased material you can't give away because it probably sounds too much like Whitesuck.

Anyway, I'm in for the Unledded project. I think we should do 'Stairway' with a zither, dulcimer, and mandocello while I sing in Old English and try to work in passages from 'Beowulf.' Do you know where my druid costume is?

Later,
Robert

I WANT TO FLY
LIKE AN EGO

LOSE CONTROL

Words and music by Kevin Federline and J. R. Rotem
Performed by Kevin Federline
Released 2006 (no chart position)

IN RECENT years a new species of celebrity has become prevalent in the pop culture landscape: the Celebri-dick.

Celebri-dicks are public figures whose fame has a direct correlation to how much of an annoying asshole they are. They're different from luminaries we "love to hate," who exaggerate brazen aspects of their personality for sheer entertainment's sake. Celebri-dicks don't play roles or pretend. They're not even famous for being famous. Celebri-dicks are famous for being fuckwads.

Not surprisingly, the best celebri-dicks are American. Nobody does the overexposed shithead routine better than us. While Paris Hilton was born a celebri-dick and fraudulent memorist James Frey lied his way into becoming one, others inherited the mantle via the laziest way possible, i.e. by banging someone even more famous than they were. This brings us to Kevin Federline, AKA KFed, who brought celebri-dickism to previously unseen heights during his brief marriage to Britney Spears. Hailing from Fresno, California, Federline's celebri-dickism began while working as a backup dancer for Britney. First he abandoned his pregnant girlfriend, actress Shar Jackson (with whom he'd already fathered a son), to get engaged to his employer. Federline then honed his celebri-dick skills by partying with his posse of slacker pals on Britney's Visa card, racing around in her sports cars, crowding her mansion with his ego, and refusing to get a job. A wannabe rapper, Federline was so ostentatious in his celebri-dickedness that I suspected it was an act, a kind of performance art that might earn him a Rockefeller Grant for acting like Vanilla Ice's autistic nephew. But after viewing his disastrous live performance of the narcissistic "Lose Control" on the 2006 Teen Choice Awards (where he uttered the phrase "black tits" to an audience of twelve-year-olds) I realized there was something far more sinister going on here.

THE SONG

Since "Lose Control" is a rap song (an oxymoron if there ever was one), there's no need for any nitpicky analysis of chords, melodies, and verse/chorus/bridge relationships. Suffice to say it contains the usual hip-hop devices like scratching, electronic drums, and subhuman bass, plus a sampled guitar sting seemingly lifted from a YouTube video of some kid demonstrating his Carlos Santana impression. The only unusual thing is some stabbing piano chords right out of an ABBA single, unusual in that they're actually played on a piano. Other than some artificial string fills zipping in and out, that's pretty much it. Production-wise, it's polished and inoffensive. Then KFed starts rapping and a new black hole appears.

Rather than doing a line-by-line analysis of the numbskull lyrics (I started but it was like killing a roach with plutonium), I instead chose to observe the celebri-dick in his natural surroundings, monitoring KFed's sneering visage on tabloid magazine covers and even watching the music video of "Lose Control" to gain insight. The video shows him preening inside a slick Hollywood night club while scores of fawning female extras dance around him adoringly, yet another form of humiliation for struggling actors.

To summarize what this, er, song's about, it's him bragging. That's it. Bragging in itself is no sin, but when it involves Kevin Federline, the result is a river of yak shit. He brags about how hip, rich, cool, talented, sexy, and famous he is, how he's a superstar, he's married to a superstar, he's welcomed into every hip club in L.A., he drives a Lamborghini and makes hit records. That's just the first stanza. He could easily stop there, but no, KFed even wants plant life to hate him.

The second set of "verses" shows him boasting about how he always wins in Vegas when playing craps, how he has dice tattooed on his wrist, how his one earring is worth more than our "budgets," how *his* Ferrari (née Britney's) is better than our cars, how nobody can't possibly spend as much money as he does, how he'll fork out $40,000 to take his friends to Miami to drink Cristal, etc. Even his tax bracket is cooler than ours. In short, KFed declares that he's better than everyone who's ever lived, including Buddha, Ghandhi, and the blonde girl who stuck her tongue down my throat back in college during a dorm party. Meanwhile, he reminds us three times how he's "the shit" and that his beats will make us "lose control." That's the entire song, beats and all.

Ordinarily anything as horrible as "Lose Control" would be my cue to unleash a salvo of nuclear shin kicking. But with KFed, I was dealing with a quantum celebri-dick, someone too obnoxious to be for real; nobody's this much of a freaking tool. I also found it telling that KFed courted so much negative attention on himself, as if he wanted to be pilloried.

That's when it all became clear to me.

WHY IT'S CREEPY

Kevin Federline is the Messiah of celebri-dicks.

That's right, readers, KFed came to Earth with a purpose: to take away the sins of other celebri-dicks like Hilton, Frey, Nicole Ritchie, oil heir Brandon Davis, the cast of *The Real Orange County*, and anybody who calls a press conference to announce that she's adopting an African baby. To accomplish this, Federline had to ditch a pregnant girlfriend, max out Britney's credit card and incur the wrath of the public. Once he transformed himself into the biggest uber-twit of modern times, all that was left was a crucifixion, which for him meant performing the worst rap song of the new millennium on a televised awards show. He didn't even lip-synch, choosing instead to rap live for maximum effect so everyone could hear him suck for real. He imploded that night and got the boot from Britney a few months later. But in the end, KFed fulfilled his destiny of absolving the sins of celebri-dicks everywhere. The next time supermodel Naomi Campbell beats up one of her maids or Brandon Davis screams "Fire crotch!" at paparazzi cameras, they can thank Federline for delaying their entrance into Hell just a little longer.

I'VE NEVER BEEN TO ME

Words and music by Ron Miller and Ken Hirsch
Performed by Charlene
Originally released 1977 (No. 97 in U.S.);
rereleased 1982 (No. 3 in U.S., No. 1 in UK)

DURING THE early to mid-nineties, I was the technical director of a well-known comedy theater company in Hollywood. Occasionally outside parties would rent the theater for stage productions, and it was from one of these bookings that I got to work with the twenty-three-year-old Daughter of a Famous American Celebrity (DOFAC), who'd come in to direct a play. While she was pleasant and easy to work with, a typical conversation with her went something like this:

DOFAC (sighing): "God, I've had a terrible day. Just terrible!"

Me: "Why? What happened?"

DOFAC: "Well, this morning I was on my way to Barry Diller's office."

Me: "The head of Fox?"

DOFAC: "Right, I had a pitch meeting. So I'm driving to the studio, my cell phone rings, and it's Michael Eisner."

Me: "The head of Disney?"

DOFAC: "Yeah. So I'm, like, 'Hey Mike, what's up?' Just then I glance in the rear-view mirror and, ohmigod, I forgot to put on eyeliner! And I've got a meeting with Barry in ten minutes! So I had to pull over, run into a Rite Aid, and buy some eyeliner. I barely made it to the meeting on time.

"I mean, it was *horrible*!"

Now, any self-respecting human listening to this would react accordingly, i.e., slap the little twit with a large flounder. I just nodded silently. *She can't help it*, I told myself. *She grew up in*

Beverly Hills. Johnny Carson bounced her on his knee. Her forgetting eyeliner on the way to meet the head of Fox is the same as me being getting kicked in the face by a deranged Clydesdale.

This was my first experience with the Pseudo-disillusioned Narcissist: a person who brags by bitching. Hollywood's full of them, pumping themselves up with tales of woe. They mention their private chalet in Aspen while complaining about a delayed plane flight. They name-drop Reese Witherspoon when describing an unpleasant dining experience. They work Matt Damon into their tirade about the service at a Mercedes dealership. What's worse, they do it intentionally so they can feel superior to you.

This brings us to "I've Never Been to Me" by the chirping pop singer Charlene. You could populate Hungary with the number of people who despise this obnoxious eighties ballad* about a whining jet setter and her "empty" life. It was first released in 1977 and flopped immediately, but it was rereleased in 1982 with a spoken bridge added to it that'd been left out of the original version. Astoundingly, it shot to No. 3 in the U.S. while hitting No. 1 in the UK. It would be the first, last, and only hit of Charlene's career, and she was consigned to the purgatory of one-hit wonders. It's an idiotic song that not even kitsch can redeem, but it is still interesting since it shows the Pseudo-disillusioned Narcissist on display. To help explain, I've written the script to a short film (there's a statute in Los Angeles that requires all residents to write shitty screenplays they'll never sell).

THE SONG

INT.RESTAURANT – NIGHT
A fancy bistro off Canon Drive in Beverly Hills. Two women are seated at a small table waiting for their food to arrive. One is

---

* It rates at No. 3 in the 1993 book *The Worst Rock 'n' Roll Records of All Time* by Jimmy Gutterman and Owen O'Donnell.

MILLIE BLAND, divorced with twelve kids, who works part-time at a head-lice treatment clinic called Nits Landing. Across from her is STARR BULLION, the richest and most famous pop singer in the world.

MILLIE

Wow, Starr, I can't believe how rich and famous you are. I wish I had your life.

STARR

Oh, Millie, Millie. If you only knew how difficult my life is.

MILLIE

Really? I'm on disability after being hit by a falling satellite. Our pit bull chewed up our car. We're about to be evicted.

STARR

But consider what I'm going through. You see, dear, I've never been to me.

MILLIE

What does that mean, Starr? Tell me.

A piano straight out of Elton John's "Tiny Dancer" softly drifts into the background. Starr stares off.

STARR

I know you're cursing about your life and you're probably a discontented mother.

MILLIE

Most of my kids are in jail. My four-year-old Benjy is doing ten years for robbing a liquor store.

STARR

So? Do you know how my life is? First, I traveled all around the country to places like Georgia and California, anywhere I could run. I had wild hot sex with a preacher and we made love in the sun.

MILLIE

I had another baby last month. He spins his head all the way around and catches flies with his tongue.

STARR

But I couldn't stay with him, Millie, because I wanted to be free and on my own. Sure, I've been to paradise but I've never been to me.

MILLIE

Then I found a scorpion nest in the basement.

STARR

Yeah, whatever. Anyway, you should know why I'm feeling so alone today. I see so much of who I used to be living in your eyes.

MILLIE

I got stung eighty-five times—

STARR

Don't interrupt. Anyway I became a big star. I traveled even more, going from Nice to the Isle of Greece. Everyone called me Jean Harlow because I looked so gorgeous.

MILLIE

The poison made my skin break out in boils—

STARR

You're interrupting again. I drank champagne on yachts while all these wealthy royals undressed me and proposed marriage. It was awful. So while I was in Monte Carlo getting oral from Leonardo Di Caprio, that's when I realized "I've never been to me."

MILLIE

Gee, I'm sorry, Starr. You must feel terrible.

STARR

I do. I mean paradise is a lie. True paradise is that baby you're holding.

MILLIE

The one with the horns? Last night he ate the cat.

STARR

Paradise is that man you argued with, the one you'll be loving tonight.

MILLIE

Jake left me for a blow-up doll.

STARR

Sometimes I cry for all the children I never had. I've spent so much of my life doing "subtle whoring."

MILLIE

How do you be a subtle whore?

STARR

The point is, Millie, I've been to paradise a million times but I've never been to me.

The piano and lounge strings fade. Starr looks at Millie.

STARR

I hope you've learned something from this, Millie. You should appreciate what you have and not the exotic jet-setting life that I lead.

MILLIE

Gosh, Starr, you're right. I guess other people might think you were a patronizing, self-absorbed bitch but I see the wisdom in your words. Thanks so much for straightening me out.

The waiter arrives with their order. A scorpion crawls out of Millie's hair and falls on her plate.

FADE TO BLACK

WHY IT'S CREEPY

While there are other songs as insipid as "I've Never Been to Me," few are as narcissistic. That's not the fault of Charlene, as she didn't write it (though her treacly performance makes it worse). What makes the song so insufferable is how we're expected to feel sorry for people like the celebrity in the song. This sort of hubris is very symptomatic of the last thirty years, when artists and songwriters started pretending to be "disillusioned" with their chosen professions while continuing to work in them. Think of all the name actors who whine about crappy Hollywood movies yet eagerly appear in them because the money's so good. Think of all the music groups who claim they have artistic integrity and independence, and then snap up the first major record contract dangled in front of them. Personally I'm all for artists getting rich and being successful. Just don't bitch about it.

As for the previously mentioned DOFAC, she knew nothing about play directing so another director was brought in to help her get the production ready (and it was awful). Today she is a well-known TV personality. I haven't seen her in years but every time a millionaire actress appearing on *The Tonight Show with Jay Leno* gives an exasperated account of finding a run in her stocking while lunching with David Geffen, I think of the DOFAC and all the lovely clueless wenches who work in her frequency.

JENNY FROM THE BLOCK

Words and music by Jennifer Lopez, Jean Claude Olivier,
Samuel Barnes, Troy Oliver, Michael Ian Oliver,
Andre Deyo, Lawrence Parker, Jason Phillips, Scott Sterling,
José Fernando Arbex Miro, and David Styles
Performed by Jennifer Lopez
Released 2002 (No. 3 in U.S., No. 3 in UK)

THERE ARE certain things I consider Rather Nots. I'd rather not eat liver. I'd rather not drive in rush-hour traffic, shove my hand into a Dumpster, or get attacked by killer bees. But I'll endure all of them if it saves me from listening to a Jennifer Lopez CD. Cranking anything by this uber-diva, be it "Waiting for Tonight" or any of the ten thousand remixes of "I'm Real" is enough to make me barf bone marrow. I appreciate her legendary bum and she was good in *Out Of Sight*, but send her albums down to Hades where they'll be appreciated better. I would've avoided the recorded Lopez catalogue but there's no way to exclude her appalling "Jenny from the Block," one of the most egregious self-love songs ever recorded.

I can recall when Lopez was so ubiquitous, you could've moved to a chamber in the Mariana Trench and still heard about her personal life: the engagement to Ben Affleck, the Bennifer phenomenon, the J. Lo moniker, the previous marriages, the relationship with Puff Daddy (before the advent of P. Diddy), ad infinitum. Lopez is currently married to salsa singer Marc Anthony, so she's learned how to ask "How come we're not in *People* magazine this week" in Spanish. Mind you, I'm not sure what to make of every rumor I've read, i.e. she demands her coffee to be stirred counterclockwise, or her entourage could fill a crop circle. She might even have screamed at a flight attendant for not having espresso available, I don't know. That she requires the scent of lilacs to be sprayed in the pathway to her dressing room, well, it's hard to believe yet not so unbelievable to have been made up. Suffice to say, if only 10 percent of the rumors about her are true, Jennifer Lopez is still a piece of work.

"Jenny from the Block" dates back to her heady Bennifer days, which explains Affleck's presence in the music video, along with rappers Jadakiss and Styles P, who up the song's hubris factor by bragging how fabulous *they* all are. Being that Lopez hails from New York's South Bronx, its backing track features a sample from the 1987 Boogie Down Productions hip-hop song "South Bronx," the sample being two guys saying "South Bronx." Apparently nobody in Lopez's camp had the wherewithal to write that.

THE SONG

"Jenny from the Block" begins with some a capella nonsense as male soul singers croon about children growing and women producing while men are either working or stealing in order to make a living. Unless appearing at the Oscars in a $25,000 Dolce & Gabbana dress classifies as "making a living," I don't know how any of this applies to Lopez. The standard drum machine and sampled guitar riff lay down a workaday dance beat while Jadakiss and Styles P rap a bunch of tired lines about her "rocks," a white T-bird, a mansion, and some homies while waiting for Lopez as she peruses the script to *Anaconda III: The Remixes*. Finally, she appears, singing the song's pseudo-humble chorus: she's still Jenny from the block and we shouldn't be fooled by the large shiny rocks that she's got. Sure, she has a lot now but she'll never forget where she came from. (Maybe she sampled the phrase "South Bronx" because she kept forgetting.)

The first verse gives us a recap of her career highlights, including her Fly Girl stint on *In Living Color*, movies, her *On the 6* album, her J. Lo phase. No mention of her demands for special lighting in recording studios or white flowers in her dressing room, or that hotel staff do not make eye contact with her. "I stayed grounded," she insists, "as the amounts roll in." Yes, that is exactly the line she says and aren't we all the better for knowing it? She also adds how "I'm really [sic] been on *Oprah*." So have three-dozen unwed mothers and the guy who wrote that fake memoir. She reminds us that there's nothing phony about her, so "don't hate." Here's an idea: don't give us a reason to.

After a repeat of the chorus, it's yet another paradoxical series of I'm-so-fantastic-at-being-humble claims. She's rockin' the biz while being in control of her career and laughing at those untrue rumors swirling around her, like the one about how Ashanti backs up most of her vocal tracks . . . OK, she'll give us that one. Lopez's most egregious claim is how she puts "God first," yet another cliche copped from hip-hop artists. (Dear rappers: Stop thanking God. He doesn't believe you.) Finally she can't and won't forget to "stay real," as real as a private hairdresser flown in from twenty-five hundred miles away to do her hair allows. For her, being real is so effortless "it's like breathing." There's a CPR joke in there somewhere.

Jadakiss and Styles P rap some more examples of her "realness" while a swarm of samples buzz around like digital horseflies. Lopez repeats the chorus one more time so we can be reminded again of how she's just "Jenny from the Block." It ends so abruptly, it sounds like Ben Affleck walked in and pulled the plug.

WHY IT'S CREEPY

Lopez has sung about her personal life so much, you'd think the FBI told her that we were interested. There's nothing wrong with being autobiographical, but if your idea of sharing is telling us how rich and fabulous you are, take two Townes Van Zant albums and call me in the morning. In fact, if she'd left out the

"I'm so grounded" claims and just kept the bragging, it might've made the song *less* offensive. What creeps me out about "Jenny from the Block" is that Lopez honestly thinks everybody should believe her. Her rep as one of the most demanding divas since Marie Antoinette is well documented, yet she releases songs like this one and "I'm Real." Recently, she tried reconnecting with her Hispanic roots by releasing an all-Spanish language album, *Como ama una mujer*. Unfortunately, she showed her "realness" by refusing to appear at any Latin music stores to do publicity, causing Ritmo Latino, a Latin music chain of fifty stores, to pull all of her CDs in protest. The all-time best was when she attended the celebrity wedding of Tom Cruise and Katie Holmes and showed up for the informal prewedding dinner in an expensive designer gown, embarrassing the modestly dressed bride-to-be. Jenny has officially left the block.

FERGALICIOUS

Words and music by Will Adams, Dani Birks,
Stacy Ann Ferguson, Juana Spirling Burns, Juanita A. Lee,
Kim R. Nazel, Derrick A. Rahming, and Shaheed Fatimah
Performed by Fergie
Released 2006 (No. 2 in U.S., No. 24 in UK)

NOTE: THE following chapter was culled from various diary entries allegedly made by hip-hop performer Stacy Ann Ferguson, AKA Fergie, in regard to her narcissistic hit "Fergalicious." The author assumes no responsibility for the authenticity of these entries—but if they aren't genuine then the guy I bought them from on eBay owes me a refund.

Sept 1, 2006
Dear Diary,
    Wow, what an exciting past few months it's been. First, the song "My Humps" with the Black Eyed Peas was a hit and all I did was rap about my ass. Then, my first solo single "London Bridge" went platinum and that was about my poonie. I really think I'm on to something.

Sept 15, 2006
    Talked to Josh D. on the phone today. He loves my Dutchess album and thinks the next single should be "Fergalicious." It's the perfect song, he reminded me, 'cuz it's about ME and how hot I am. What a great idea! I bet it'll be as big as "Let's Get Retarded" with just as positive a message.

THE SONG
Sept 25, 2006
    I hate hate hate the music critic from the Trafalgar Weekly Gazette. He listened to an advanced copy of "Fergalicious" and called it "pure hubris." I'd be even more

pissed off if I knew what it meant. But what does he know? He doesn't realize the work Will and me put into recording it. I mean, it took us almost a full hour. Like, first we had to write the music so we picked J. J. Fad's "Supersonic" and used it 'cuz there's a law that says you can't write your own music anymore. Then we chose a drum and synth loop from the Garage Band program on Will's laptop and sampled the strings from "Papa Was a Rolling Stone" by some group called the Titillations or something. All that alone took us nearly twenty minutes.

When we got to the lyrics, Will asked me, "Yo, what part of your body haven't we rubbed in everyone's face?" I said, how about all of me at once? It won't just be about my bum and love tunnel. It'll be about my boobies, bung hole, and pee shaft, too. I can talk about how delicious I am. No wait, instead of delicious, I could be Fergalicious. ~~Will liked it and said he never thought of me as an adjective before. After I Googled~~ "adjective" and figured out he hadn't dissed me, I told him thanks.

Recording it was a blast, and easy too. You know how they say you should always tell the truth in a song? Well, I sure do that in "Fergalicious." Everyone knows that boys jerk themselves blind whenever they see my picture in *Spin* or *Blender* magazine. See, they all want my "treasure" but, uh-uh, they can't have it. Nobody's allowed to touch me, all they can do is look as long as they don't make eye contact. I tease boys because they come and go like the seasons, y'know, like Spring, August, and Wednesday.

I really like the hook where I call myself Fergalicious. But that don't mean I'm easy. No, sir, I don't have to be. All I gotta do is blow kisses at guys and they immediately stain their jeans with boy batter. They'll even line up and down the block just to "watch what I got." God, I'm so Fergalicious!

In the song, I talk about how some guys have the nerve to call me by my real name. "Hey, Stacy" they say. I hate that so I have to remind them I'm Fergie, spelled "F to the E, R, G, the I, the E." One guy said, "Wouldn't it be easier to spell it F-E-R-G-I-E?" I shot him.

How do I look this awesome? I work out all the time. Like, I mention how I'm always in the gym doing "my fitness" and then more boys line up on the block waiting for me to come out. Seriously, you can see the pools of jizz on the sidewalk. I'm just so Fergalicious.

Will made me sing during one part. It was kind of hard since I had to hit notes and stuff. But I got into it because I sang more truthful stuff about me, like how if you're really patient or you run a successful group that needs a white chick with great knockers, I might get with you. And boy, are you in for a treat 'cuz I'm tasty (I had Will rap how tasty I am. I had to keep reminding him to spell it right, T-A-S-T-E-Y).

The final part of "Fergalicious" was cool because I got to rap really really fast to all the ladies that I'm not trying to steal their men. You know I get that all the time. For a joke, I added that I'm probably coming off a little bit conceited. I still think that it's funny because, seriously, who'd believe it?! Will ends it by spelling "delicious" over and over. Of course, he's talking about me.

WHY IT'S CREEPY

Nov. 4, 2006

Sorry, diary, for taking so long to write. It's been a great last few weeks. "Fergalicious" is a big hit and reached #2 here in the U.S. We have such great taste in music! I knew it would do well and why shouldn't it? I mean, it's an honest song with not a single original piece of music in it so we won't get into any trouble. A few asshole reviewers thought the song was narcissistic and it made some lists as Worst Song of 2006. They said it's more of a novelty song than a serious hip-hop track and I'm in danger of becoming an annoyance. They're just jealous because none of them are Fergalicious like I am. Come to think of it, I'm really the only one who's Fergalicious. Even when I break wind, it smells like lilacs.

Well, gotta run, diary. I'm heading for my workout to get more fitness. Funny, but my instructor told me I can't get fitness. I have to do fitness in order to get fit. So I shot him.

LOVE'S JUST
ANOTHER WORD FOR
I WANT TO EAT YOUR
LIVER

COME TO MY WINDOW

Words and music by Melissa Etheridge
Performed by Melissa Etheridge
Released 1994 (No. 13 in U.S.)

JEWEL, ALANIS Morissette, Sarah McLachlan, Jann Arden, Joan Osborne, Meredith Brooks, Suzanne Vega, Sheryl Crow, Shawn Colvin . . . The nineties was to be the era of Chicks with Acoustic Instruments (CHAI) until they were replaced by Chicks with Obnoxious Manager Parents (CHOMP). This change was a corporate decision made because music industry moguls finally figured out that guys are afraid of female singer/songwriters. We'd rather see a dozen gun-wielding ninjas attack an orphanage than a woman with an acoustic guitar walk into a room. Give us a bimbo who needs four gigabytes worth of studio processing to make her sing in tune. It's less pressure.

After the CHOMPs evicted them from the sorority house, the CHAIs carried on to various levels of success. Melissa Etheridge has endured the longest; her debut album appeared in 1987 and she's managed to stay relevant in a notoriously fickle industry. What I've noticed is that her substantial catalogue is built on personal suffering and consuming human flesh. Many of her songs feature her drowning in her desire, shocking and electrifying someone, tasting her sweat, quenching her thirst, feeling the steel of red-hot truth, and enduring nights of lust and fire while asking to be stripped and cut until she bleeds. This means she likes you.

I'm not attacking Ms. Etheridge. She's a prolific songwriter with a soulful voice and she gets extra kudos for her successful battle with cancer. But Melissa still took the Chicks with Acoustic Instruments paradigm to a carnivorous level and I suspect it's partially due to her instrument of choice, an Ovation twelve-string guitar. It's easy to recognize an Ovation; it has a patented bowl-shaped body that allows it to replicate the sound of scarab beetles being bitch-slapped inside a Tupperware bowl. I've seen many aspiring songwriters perform self-autopsy songs at coffeehouses and most of them used Ovations plugged directly into the PA system, creating the ugliest guitar sound in the world. Listening to Melissa Etheridge means hearing a lot of Ovation guitars and first-person narrative; over a dozen of her songs feature "I" in the title alone. One of her most intense compositions is "Come to My Window," which has become an anthem among lesbians. The song appears on 1994's *Yes I Am*, her first CD release after coming out as a gay woman, and there are any number of people who swear the track's title is a veiled reference to oral sex. If someone wants to confirm this with her, be my guest.

THE SONG

Depending on where you cue it up, "Come to My Window" has two introductions to it. The first one opens the song, being a funereal organ over which Melissa slowly sings the chorus. Radio stations usually skip past it when playing "Come to My Window," as does Melissa when performing it live. Therefore so will I.

When the band kicks into a medium-tempo rock beat, you can hear the song's impending drama in the instruments, including her nervous twelve-string. The opening verse has Melissa revealing how she calls us just to "listen to your breath" (or listen to someone say "Hello? Who is this? Stop calling me!"). That's fine, but the next line has her descending into Hell to "hold the hand of Death." Jeez, a trip to Hell? Flowers would've sufficed. The rest of the stanza shows that she'll stop at nothing to ease her "precious ache," adding that we don't know how much she can endure. Well, she's been to Hell, so we have an idea.

The song's anthemic chorus is considered an enciphered

invitation for some girl-on-girl tongue action (you can guess what the "window" is). I admit I never thought of it that way when the song was first released; I'm always behind in my euphemisms. But then you have to contend with the line "Crawl inside, wait by the light of the moon." How large is this window anyway? The second stanza shows her as an insomniac who can't let herself sleep, which sets up the rhyme of making promises she's unable to "keep," like buying a better guitar. The next line is another whiplash declaration, however, as she describes the "blackness that has seeped into my chest" and how she needs us in her blood. So now the tally includes Hell, the hand of Death, blackness, seeping chests, and blood. Sounds like Slayer to me.

After a repeat of the chorus, the bridge emphasizes her defiance of public opinion, declaring how she doesn't care what anyone thinks of their love. I'm only wondering how she got in and out of Hell so easily. The chorus finishes the song with the phrase "I'm comin' home" echoing in the listener's ears.

WHY IT'S CREEPY

"Come to My Window" is one of Melissa Etheridge's finer vocal performances, well delivered without a hint of false drama, while the song rocks musically. What pushes it into creepy territory are the zero-to-sixty confessions in the verse sections, where confession A is totally usurped by confession B. It's more obvious when you break it down:

VERSE No. 1
A. She makes a phone call.
B. She goes to Hell and holds hands with Death.

VERSE No. 2
A. She has insomnia.
B. She has a seeping chest of blackness and needs us flowing through her blood.

This is a common lyrical device in many CHAI songs and I've never quite understood it. Do people ever confess to things this way?

A. I forgot to pick up the dry cleaning.
B. I slept with your sister and joined the Nazi party.

Some older readers may remember "Come to My Window" for its notorious music video featuring a schizoid Juliette Lewis locked up in an institution with bandages on her wrists following a suicide attempt. Filmed in greyish-blue colors, ~~Lewis cries, laughs, scribbles on the walls, has imaginary~~ conversations, and even recites the opening verse, including the hand-holding Grim Reaper stuff in a whimpering voice. (The experience must've rendered her insane as she now fronts her own band, Juliette and the Licks.) Watching the video only enhances the song's creepiness, and the melodramatic scenario doesn't help. But then again, I'm a guy and Melissa's a CHAI. Maybe I'm just afraid of her.

POSSESSION

Words and music by Sarah McLachlan
Performed by Sarah McLachlan
Released 1993 (No. 73 in U.S.)

WHENEVER I hear Sarah McLachlan's music, I think of candles. Lots and lots of candles. Enough candles to be seen from condo balconies on Neptune. Magical candles that never start fires or melt hot wax all over the top of a $50,000 Steinway piano, which is where you'll find them in the first place.

I'm thinking of Sarah McLachlan's depressing song "Angel," yet another SAG-waiver casting of heavenly beings in a pagan production. Find any TV or video clip of her singing "Angel" and you'll see an autumn harvest of candles burning around her like a biblical plague of fireflies. Meanwhile, she's dressed in black on a black, black stage, her pale face floating above her piano like an orb. If she weren't such an attractive woman, I'd swear she was Nosferatu.

But I digress. We're here to examine Sarah's creepy love song "Possession," her first hit single that introduced her ethereal music to the masses. Although it only reached No. 73 on the U.S. charts, "Possession" is still in regular rotation on adult contemporary radio stations and a favorite among her formidable fan base. While Sarah McLachlan was a major force during the nineties' CHAI era (she conceived Lilith Fair), she reminds me more of AC/DC, in that they both keep releasing the same album over and over again. As for her music, people either find it moving and captivating or fall asleep during earthquakes while listening to it. For me, it depends on how her hair looks. If she's got those long, sexy raven locks spilling past her shoulders, I'm there. If she's sporting the ultra-short haircut that Janine Turner wore on TV's *Northern Exposure*, I'm in a deep snooze.

"Possession" was the very first Sarah McLachlan song I ever heard, courtesy of the MTV music video. I remember watching it while thinking, wow, what a babe, what a great voice, what's with all the candles? Then I listened to the lyrics and an unsettling feeling came over me. For a love song, it was pretty intense. She sounds like a stalker. It was only later that I learned the story behind "Possession" (which McLachlan fans already know) involving lawsuits, accusations of plagiarism, and a stalker.

~~In 1991, Sarah McLachlan was a twenty-four-year-old rising~~ star in her native Canada and had just released her second album, *Solace*, when she drew the unwanted attention of a computer programmer named Uwe Vandrei who'd become obsessed with her. For the next three years, Vandrei bombarded her with hundreds of letters and e-mails that were alternately impassioned and threatening. When he started following her around, McLachlan was forced to hire a bodyguard and even get a restraining order issued against Vandrei. Meanwhile, the ordeal inspired her to write the first-person song "Possession" about the mind and motives of a stalker.

When her third album, *Fumbling Towards Ecstasy*, was released in 1993, "Possession" was its lead single, and it went to No. 1 in Canada as well as charting in the U.S. Vandrei heard "Possession" and went, *hmm, that obsessed, panting freak she's singing about sounds like me.* In one of the most bizarre civil cases ever filed, Vandrei sued McLachlan, claiming she'd plagiarized passages from his psychotic letters to her and used them in the song's lyrics. He demanded $250,000 in royalties and a face-to-face meeting with her on television to "discuss" the song (back then, this was unthinkable). The case never went to trial because, in a tragic twist to the story, Uwe Vandrei committed suicide in 1994.

THE SONG

There are two versions of "Possession," one of them a solo piano and voice arrangement that's gained a following over the years. I opted for the original full-group version because it's far darker and I've had enough of Sarah-at-the-piano with "Angel" and "I Will Remember You" to last me a sea turtle's lifetime. It begins with a Hammond organ playing High Mass chords that don't ever quite resolve (think "Amen" being sung "Ahhhh-Mennnn-Ahhh . . ."). It's deliberate and seems to suggest the unsettled mind of someone who cannot focus. Sarah's airy voice sets up a desolate landscape where a wind blows "across the great divide," while voices and memories are trapped. She creates the persona of a lonely insomniac who calls the night his companion and solitude his guide. The question he obsesses over is whether he can spend the rest of his life not being satisfied. Apparently, his satisfaction requires chloroform and a small cage.

The rest of the band steps in with a muted pulsing beat as Sarah goes into the creepy chorus. The stalker protagonist overwhelms us with promises to hold us down and kiss us hard, suggesting he's unfamiliar with the term "personal space." After taking our breath away, he says he'll wipe our tears away while we close our eyes.

If the disturbed Uwe Vandrei is the one being characterized here, this might explain why he was a computer programmer. If you work in an office and your computer goes haywire, does the IT department ever send over anyone normal to fix it? No, you always get the grumbling misanthrope with the *X-Men* comics collection who waddles to your cubicle a week later and accuses you of overloading your RAM.

The next stanza gets more unsettling as McLachlan's hunter-gatherer gripes bitterly about being betrayed in a world where he stumbles around, tripping over hard drives and printer cables. He cannot find "an honest word" from anyone and thinks the truth is "enslaved." This is the sort of self-pity that the socially stunted display around others, where they become Travis Bickle wannabes and base their friendships on how much the other person feigns interest in their JFK assassination theory. But now he's got his eye on this new Canadian singer with the dark hair and hypnotic voice. Her songs speak to him in riddles and rhymes, and he wants to inhale her exhalations. He just can't figure out why she won't answer the 497 letters he sent her last week.

After a second pass through the holding/kissing/breath-stealing chorus, there is a brief "jam" featuring an actual electric guitar solo, a rare commodity in a Sarah McLachlan song. Finally, the stalker realizes dawn is approaching. While he loves the isolation of night, it's "morning that I dread." Daylight means more work, more DOS bullshit, more requests for expanded memory, and more people who flee the break room every time he enters it. The only escape from this hellhole is *her*. Nothing stands between the two of them being together and he won't be denied.

The chorus returns and he makes his promise one last time to hold her down and kiss her hard enough to lock teeth. The song ends on an unresolved musical phrase, with the organ fading off into the great divide.

WHY IT'S CREEPY

"Possession" is one of the most sublime creepy love songs ever recorded and it floats past the ears of those who don't take note of the lyrics at first listen. I was taken aback by it when I first heard it because the organ was Procul Harum freaky and the lyrics to the chorus were too off-kilter to be dismissed as a touch-feely love song. When I later learned about McLachlan's troubles with Vandrei and his subsequent suicide, it explained a lot and gave a perverse subtext to "Possession." But even if the song had sprung entirely from McLachlan's imagination, it would still keep you on the edge of your seat. It's one of the best things she's ever done.

While listening to "Possession," which I hadn't heard in years, I also revisited the music video. The candles were still there, as well as the goth-lite ambience and Sarah's floor-length black gown. Her hair was long (yay) and her angelic face looked the same then as it does now, fifteen years later, giving it a Dorian Grey aspect that's almost as creepy as the song. The video incorporates voyeuristic images of McLachlan displayed on waving sheets from a film projector, probably similar to the hazy images of McLachlan that Uwe Vandrei played in his head during the three years he stalked her. It makes "Possession" that much more disturbing.

While Sarah McLachlan has never been as self-indulgent as her contemporaries Sophie B. Hawkins and the intolerable Paula Cole, she's been criticized even by her fans for relying too much on blase songs with formulaic relationship themes. She's not a great melodist and the power in her music tends to come from her extraordinary voice. I wish she'd venture more into the dark side, because "Possession" is still as captivating now as it was in 1993. While she doesn't have to be Soundgarden, it wouldn't hurt for her to rock out a little more, too. Please, Sarah, no more songs about angels and memories played on the piano. And don't cut your hair.

BABY LOVE

Words and music by Joan Osborne, Anthony J. Petruzzelli,
Erik Della Penna, and Rainy Orteca
Performed by Joan Osborne
Released 2000 (no chart position)

FOR MOTOWN fans who might be reading this book, this chapter is not about the famous and charming Supremes hit "Baby Love," but rather about a putrid song with the same title by singer Joan Osborne. So bad is this adult-teacher-seduces-young-student number that it commits one of the worst musical crimes ever: ruining perfectly good music with bad engineering and worse lyrics.

Born in Kentucky in 1962, Joan Osborne made a splash in 1995 with her CD *Relish*, which featured the hit single "One of Us," built around a guitar figure that resembles a twelve-year-old learning Bach on a Telecaster. The song's rhetorical chorus "What if God was one of us" became so ubiquitous on radio and MTV that God's attorneys eventually called demanding that she cease and desist. Osborne pushed the envelope more with her follow-up single, the erotically charged "Right Hand Man," a reworking in 7/4 time of Captain Beefheart's grinding "Clear Spot." (She references her panties being in a wad. Enough said.) A soulful singer when she wants to be, her music videos showcased her sultriness, Raphaelite curls, and nose ring the size of a manhole cover. Following the success of *Relish*, Osborne waited nearly five years before releasing her next CD, *Righteous Love*, which contains "Baby Love," easily the worst song on the entire album yet the one that ended up being released as the single.

According to Joan herself, "Baby Love" is "inspired" by the notorious case of Mary Kay Letourneau, an attractive thirty-four-year-old schoolteacher from Washington State who in 1997 was caught having a sexual affair with a thirteen-year-old male student in her class. Granted, such a liaison is the fantasy of many pubescent schoolboys, but the scandal made national news when Letourneau became pregnant with the boy's child. It didn't help that she was already married with four children. The case ended with Letourneau serving seven months in prison, and on her release she quickly violated her parole by reuniting with the boy and getting pregnant a second time. Such sordid behavior might be fodder for a roman à clef or even a cheeky They Might Be Giants song, but not a Joan Osborne single. Grotesque humor is normally not the bailiwick of CHAI artists.

THE SONG

"Baby Love" opens with a serviceable rock vamp right out of a .38 Special studio session (listen to "Caught Up in You" for clarification). As stated before, there's nothing wrong with the music to "Baby Love," although it plays up its roots-rock conceit a tad much (producers: don't bring a sixties Farfisa organ to any recording session unless you plan to set it on fire). Otherwise the band riffs along nicely, the drums are great, the guitar is funky, then . . . the lyrics kick in.

The first felony to occur in "Baby Love" is Joan's vocals. For no logical reason, the engineer filters her normally powerful voice so that it sounds as though she's whispering into a mobile phone (now there's a waste of calling minutes). If this was meant to pay homage to late-night phone calls between Letourneau and her boy lover, it's too obscure and plain stupid. It's like handing a ukulele to Eddie Van Halen.

"Tender as a peach," she coos disturbingly, setting up the on-the-nose rhyme of "love to teach" in the second line. We learn that her affair with her young charge began as a lazy little poke. Thanks, now we've got that visual in our minds. However, we discover that by the next day, she's hopelessly smitten and that her ears have started to bleed, probably from hearing the playback of her vocals.

The chorus of "I'm in baby love" is repeated over and over again, efficiently upping the ick factor of the song. A blatting baritone sax underpins it, while the reedy Farfisa throws in a "Three Blind Mice" fill. When the second verse arrives, the filtering effect on her vocals thankfully disappears, but that doesn't help much as Joan sings as though she's *imitating* she's on a mobile phone. In this stanza, the lyrics turn somewhat confusing as she claims she was innocent while asking the boy what happened to his manners (he's thirteen years old; he's not supposed to have manners). Evidently, news of their arrangement has gotten out, because there are references to being dragged through the dirt and the potential for blood being spilled. Still, she can't imagine that he'd ever leave her. Then the banal yet creepy chorus, "I'm in baby love again . . ."

By the third stanza, you're pretty much over this storyline, while Joan's still singing through the mobile phone (hang the hell up, already). This is where the clumsy metaphors found in many CHAI songs appear, as Joan pleads for him to take her in his "fist" so that he can watch her body "melt away." She acknowledges that he's a victim of her appetite, yet asks him if he's willing to be the man in the relationship, shaving optional. We endure the chorus one more time, hearing her plaintively wailing about being in baby love agaaaiinnn! . . . until it fades.

WHY IT'S CREEPY

To be honest, I wasn't aware of the background story to "Baby Love" when it was initially released. All I thought when I first heard the song on the radio was that this new Joan Osborne single sucks rocks. I also thought my speakers were damaged because, geez, her voice sounded awful. Whatever pretensions she exhibited in her interviews, i.e. looking off-camera from the corners of the eyes, you could forgive her because she looked great in her videos, could really belt, and had the nerve to rework Captain Beefheart. That all disappeared after "Baby Love" rolled out on the airwaves. Even disregarding the Letourneau data, the song is plain unpleasant to listen to, what with the vocals-via-Nokia and her cooing about a little poke with some kid who's tender as a peach. Not surprisingly, "Baby Love" quickly took a nosedive in the charts, taking *Righteous Love* with it. If she'd changed the lyrics and fired the engineer, she might've had another hit, not a reverse version of *Lolita*. She acquitted herself somewhat as a guest vocalist for the Grateful Dead in 2003, but her solo career has yet to recover.

FEELIN' LOVE

Words and music by Paula Cole
Performed by Paula Cole
Released 1996 (no chart position)

For those who've forgotten her, Paula Cole was the most cliched member of the nineties' CHAI movement, best known for her overplayed "I Don't Want to Wait," the theme to the teenage TV drama *Dawson's Creek* (the song became so maddening that it caused series star James Van Der Beek to think he was a good actor). Yet that track is "Hollaback Girl" compared to the emotional bloodletting one encounters in the rest of her song catalog. You could always rely on Cole to adopt the Angry Militant Feminist stereotype that most of her CHAI colleagues tried to avoid, like when she threw a fit after a magazine airbrushed out her armpit hair in a photo (true). Politically correct to the point of being obsessive, Paula railed against straight males who earned more than $40,000 a year and could find racism in a can of black olives.

In my list of neutering experiences, including watching *Waiting to Exhale* while sober, listening to Paula Cole's *This Fire* album ranks near the top. Besides "I Don't Want to Wait," this CD contains an ample number of penis-hacking, primal-screaming bipolar songs that show how she doesn't just have "issues," she has lifetime subscriptions; her meltdown at the end of "Nietzsche's Eyes" is something one must hear to believe. It's on *This Fire* that I found the innocuously titled "Feelin' Love," a song that leaves the listener feelin' somethin' else.

THE SONG
"Feelin' Love" is performed in a vocal style uncommon to CHAI

songs, that being pornographic. It opens with a venereal groove of molasses-tempo drums, loping bass, and Fender Rhodes piano straight out of a porn loop* (if there'd been a wah-wah guitar, I really would've gotten suspicious). After eight bars, Paula comes in with a high, gasping vocal that sounds as though she's singing inside an iron lung. I'm officially labeling this technique as "soprano-berculosis."

Right away the listener is pulled into simile hell in the opening verse, where she says *you* make her feel like a "sticky pistil leaning into her stamen." For those who slept through biology at school, the pistil and stamen are the female and male parts of a flower. When pollen from the stamen is transferred to the pistil, the plant reproduces. Leave it to this woman to make pollination sound dirty.

As the song sleazily gropes along, we hear how she feels like "Mr. Sunshine" and "splendor in the grass," making it the only time that LSD and an old Warren Beatty film have appeared together in the same sentence. But the real jaw-dropping clincher comes when she reveals how she feels like the Amazon River is "running between my thighs." Having endured as much twisted music as I have over the years, I've heard my share of grotesque lyrics, yet I'm unable to find a line that tops this one. Does anyone need to know that Paula Cole has a South American tributary in her pelvic area? The chorus is inane, consisting of her repeating how she feels "love love love love love love love" until it drives you nuts nuts nuts nuts. Meanwhile, she's still singing like an asthmatic mezzo-soprano.

Having already grossed us out with her vaginal Brazilian metaphor, she goes on to describes herself as being a candy apple, all "red and horny," before dispensing with her feminist ardor to become a "dumb blonde" who waits in the doorway with her

---

* "Feelin' Love" can be found in something far worse, namely the soundtrack to the awful 1998 Meg Ryan film *City of Angels*.

breasts showing through her tight, wet T-shirt until one of us charges in, ties her to the bed, and ravishes her. (You go first. No, really, I don't mind.) If these graphic carnal descriptions are meant to be erotic, I'm not sure what self-help book Paula read to get her ideas. ("When seducing a man, be sure to tell him you're a horny apple and that you have the world's longest river running in your birth canal.") The chorus returns to bug the shit shit shit shit out of us while we look around for the waiter so we can pay the dinner tab and run like hell.

The bridge, all woozy from doing tequila shots, has Paula asking herself rhetorical questions like whether she's Barry White or just "hot inside?" (Or maybe you're a big freak.) The song concludes with a coda of moonlight references along with a vow that she'll be our death—which I totally believe, by the way.

WHY IT'S CREEPY

Besides all the grotesque descriptions, there's something very disingenuous about "Feelin' Love," more like a parody of R-rated pillow talk (and I suspect that's what it is), i.e. "This is the kind of submissive trash men like to hear." This isn't a bad idea, but in order to work, a sense of humor is required and Paula Cole is not exactly a bundle of chuckles. Too much of her work is either overly bitter or overly confessional, sometimes even overly bitterly confessional. After enduring vitriolic songs on *This Fire* like "Throwing Stones" ("You call me bitch . . . I call you liar"), hearing a stamen-seduces-a-pistil analogy is just plain unconvincing. Plus, I'll never watch a Discovery Channel special about the Amazon the same way ever again.

Although Paula Cole is a technically gifted singer and musician, and her music can be soulful and funky at times, it struggles under the weight of her lyrics and vocal histrionics. Paula allowed her Elektra-like muse to overwhelm her talent while arming too many of her songs with battleaxes when a butter knife would've been sufficient.

BREAK ME

Words and music by Jewel Kilcher
Performed by Jewel
Released 2002 (No. 30 in U.S.)

FOR YEARS I've wanted to take a crack at writing poetry. It doesn't seem too hard since most contemporary poetry is just

> *sentences that are*
> *formatted to look*
> *like*
> *this which helps make them*
> *look more*
> *poetic*

Then again, I could imitate Jewel and

> *reach into my soul where my barren*
> *heart yearns for the*
> *fleeting brush of*
> *an angel's wing and my breasts,*
> *my mounds of tactile temptation,*
> *swell with the milk of a thousand mothers who*
> *suckle their infants under a*
> *night sky of diamonds,*
> *and not those icky diamonds from Africa dug up by*
> *exploited workers.*

Jewel is an acquired taste and she mostly appeals to teenage white girls who draw unicorns in their notebooks and fail to see the irony in collecting Hello Kitty bags. While I find her songs to be as wispy as her voice, I normally don't think they're creepy because she's never gone the Paula Cole route by singing about stamens that rape pistils. On the other hand, she did write the line "I break the yolks and make a smiley face," which I always wait for like an impending car accident every time "You Were Meant for Me" comes on the radio. Granted, Jewel was nineteen when she penned it, but she's never strayed too far from that kind of earnestness, and the older she gets, the more unsettling it becomes. This may be why her love ballad "Break Me" from 2002 sounds so creepily oddball.

THE SONG

"Break Me" has a promising start with a grunge guitar slowly playing haunting chords, avoiding the folky acoustic intros to most of her songs. But, Lord, after the brushed drums, bass, and piano come in, she starts singing and it's sibilance central. Her vocals are so cracked and whispery, she sounds like a Jewel impressionist, albeit one who doesn't like Jewel.

OK, poetry break:

> *The soprano's voice sifts and warbles like*
> *the hiss*
> *of a gasping balloon whose*
> *chamber was filled with*
> *the*
> *breath of an innocent*
> *child birthed*
> *by a flaxen winged*
> *angel with breasts of velveteen*

Jewel sings of wanting to meet someone in a place where the light "lends itself to soft repose" (kinda picky, aren't we?). She tells him he can undress her, but warns that she is thorny like a rose (as opposed to being horny like an apple). Hmm, reposing light and a naked body covered with thorns. Can't we just drink some beer and make out? "You could hurt me" with bare hands or with sharp words, she sings, but she's lost to him now and there's nothing that can save her from it. The chorus (actually, the choooooorrrrrrussss because it's ssssooooooooo ssslllllowwwwww) has Jewel asking him to "break me" and "take me," anything to feel his arms again.

> *Your fleshy pistons*
> *embrace my shimmering shell like*
> *the simian peeling*
>
> *a*
>
> *gossamer*
> *breadfruit with its*
> *monstrous palms of*
> *hairy digits*
> *O that you might crush my*
> *spine. Cripple me, you ape you.*

The next stanza features one of Jewel's fuzzier analogies, as she feels as though she's underwater, where she's "let go and lost control." As we've gone from reposing light and thorny roses to similes for drowning, I'm guessing she selects her metaphors like produce at supermarkets. She also sings about how "water kisses" fill her mouth, so either the marine metaphor is getting away from her or she's dating a diver. Haiku break:

> *I love the strong man*
> *with the round metal helmet*
> *and bubbly air hose*

After an unnecessary bridge during which she requests to be kissed a couple of times, the chorus returns and she whispers her desire for him to break her and take her, in that order. "Just let me feel your love again . . ." The grunge-light guitar, piano, and rhythm section slow to a crawl behind her and she curls up to a close.

> *So as the day waves nighty-night*
> *To the night*
> *I don my nightie and*
> *say nighty-night*
> *to the knot in*
> *my*
> *knee.*

WHY IT'S CREEPY

Jewel's songs focus a lot on relationships, not unusual for a singer/songwriter, but there's often something a little clingy about them. She hasn't been a feverish teenager for a while, yet "Break Me," its post-grunge production aside, sounds exactly like the Dear Diary tracks she wrote for her first album when she was nineteen. Therein lies the creepiness of "Break Me," in that you can take the Alaskan-born singer out of high school but the opposite scenario fails to take hold. I would think a mature woman in her thirties would want to eschew the flighty courting that teenagers do and instead focus on real feelings and real conflicts. Instead, Jewel works up her jones for poetry and starts loading the imagery cannon.

> *My bazooka of rhyme and verse*
> *is no curse*
> *like the ammo in my purse*
> *which is worse*
> *because it may burst*
> *and blow off my foot*
> *I go, owwie! Owwie!*

I'm sure Jewel means well but the thorny rose, reposing light, and bewildering water kisses only force the average guy confronted with her analysis of their relationship to search for a polite way to ask, "What the hell are you babbling about?" Her wounded whispering vocals resemble a summer stock actress performing Ophelia's dying soliloquy in *Hamlet*.

Jewel's coffeehouse roots have grown into a big, shady tree over the years, so no matter how much she's experimented with house music and old jazz stylings, she'll always be the cute blonde alt-folkie who used to live in her van. That's not a bad thing, but the older she gets, the more her older material becomes dated and she'll need fresh songs that coincide at least somewhat with her actual age. Songs like "Break Me" sound like the product of an adolescent's journal, but when they come from the pen of a thirty-something Jewel, it's time she moved out of the van and got an apartment. (Yes, that's a metaphor, too. Sorry, but I've been listening to this woman all day.)

I'M NOT BITTER,
I JUST WISH YOU'D
DIE, YOU
MISERABLE PIG

YOU OUGHTA KNOW

Words and music by Alanis Morissette and Glen Ballard
Performed by Alanis Morissette
Released 1995 (No. 6 in U.S., No. 22 in UK)

NOW THAT we're all familiar with the CHAI acronym, let's apply it to Alanis Morissette back in her *Jagged Little Pill* days. Chick with Anxious Insecurity? How about Chick with Advanced Insanity? Maybe it's Chick with Assassination Instructions. Like most people, I'd never heard of Ms. Morissette until her castrating betrayal anthem "You Oughta Know" came shooting out of my car radio like an estrogen cannon ball one day in 1995. The song was everywhere that summer, and for three months guys couldn't get laid. Instead, men who hadn't spoken to their ex-girlfriends in years heard bitter messages left on their answering machines. Some found obscenities scrawled in lipstick on their car windshields. Me, I was dating a lawyer who hated her father. I was screwed regardless.

A former teenage dance/pop performer in her native Canada, Alanis Morissette reinvented herself as an edgy alternative artist with her gazillion-selling third album *Jagged Little Pill*, which features the notorious "You Oughta Know." Cultural pundits anointed her the Angry White Female of the nineties—which, to be fair, wasn't entirely accurate. She could also be optimistic in her songs ("Head Over Feet"), but "You Oughta Know" banged around the cerebrum so hard it rendered listeners somewhat oblivious to her total persona, especially if they were male.

THE SONG
I knew that to do justice to this song, I'd have to enter Ms. Morissette's cerebrum and poke around. I confess I feel a little

intrusive digging into the part of her psyche that created "You Oughta Know," because:

1. I'm treading on the long-buried torment of an angry, betrayed woman.
2. Everybody in the freaking world has heard this song a million times.

Anyway, I'm here now, inside the part of Alanis Morissette's head where all the *Jagged Little Pill* files are kept. I can't tell you how I gained entry except that it required a six-pack of Moosehead and saying "hoser" to the right people. I'm surrounded by hundreds of journals, old VHS copies of *Full House*, and a set of bloodstained hedge clippers. I can hear the uneasy skipping of a snare drum and pithy bass fills while she's wishing some guy well, saying she's happy for them and only wants the best for them both. OK, this seems rather cordial and understanding—whoa, the lights just changed. It's all purple and red now, the official colors of pissed off. A crunching rock guitar slams a chord while visions from past encounters fly about. She's asking if the other woman is "perverted" like she was. Oh, Lord, I see flashing images of Alanis giving a hummer to some guy inside a darkened cinema while *Look Who's Talking* is playing (no wonder she's not watching). Now she's asking if the other woman is willing to have his baby.

I'm on the floor now, covering my head as long, strung-together verses scream above "theloveyougave . . . ablemakeit . . . beopenwide . . . NO! . . . speakhername . . . toldmeholdme till ya diedDIED." Wow, it's just like the record. Now I see her standing on a large, flesh-colored pipe while sporting talons for teeth as she points out the mess he left when he went away. Wait, now she has a cross, which she waves about like Van Helsing. "You oughta know," she screams.

The lights dim slightly. The alt-rock music track calms down while I hear her commenting on how peaceful he seems. She's not, however, and felt he should know . . . BAM! The purple-red lighting fills the chamber. She's calling him Mr. Duplicity while her journals flap about like crows. His quick replacement of her was "a slap in the face," but she asks him if he thinks about her while the two of them are screwing (probably not, but I'm not gonna tell her).

Uh-oh, gotta hit the floor again. "Theloveyougave . . . ablemakeit . . . beopenwide . . . NO! . . . speakhername . . . toldmeholdme tillya diedDIED." How does she spit all those words out without dislocating her uvula? I'm hearing that the bastard is still alive. There goes the chorus. The pipe she's standing on is bigger now, rounder, fuller. It seems to swell in size while tilting up. Oh my, she's bashing the pipe with the cross, causing it to sag and shrink in size. "It's not fair to deny me!" she screams. "You oughta know!"

The lights go out. I'm left in a pitch-black chamber while the music eases. I hear wordless vocals echoing about the room, part Siren, part menstrual cramp. They get louder and louder. "Ayyyee ayyyyyeeee . . ." The lights flash back on, blood-red in color now, the color of emasculation. I hit the floor again as more scattershot run-on phrases fly over my head: "Cuzthejoke . . . laidbed . . . notgonnfade . . . closeeyes . . . youKNOWIT! . . . scratchmynails . . . downback . . . hopeyafeelit . . . FEELIT!!" The room explodes in fire as I glimpse Alanis on top of the fleshy pipe as she smashes it to a bloody pulp with the cross. She's screaming about being denied, bearing the cross, and dammit, "YOU OUGHTA KNOW."

It ends abruptly. The lights return to dim amber. I look around to see the journals torn up and shredded, the *Full House* tapes splintered and unraveled, and fresh blood on the hedge clippers. I take my leave of Alanis's head, stealing a couple of towels on the way out.

WHY IT'S CREEPY

There's nothing more terrifying to men than a woman's anger, especially if there's a good reason for it. There's a fair amount of inimitable truth to "You Oughta Know," except for the cinema fellatio bit. No guy can get a girl to do that anymore. Why do you think cinema box-office receipts are declining? While the passage of time has somewhat dulled the, ahem, jagged edge of "You Oughta Know," it's still a mesmerizing song, albeit a creepy one to the average Joe. Almost any man will wince at the sheer mention of this tune while instinctively placing his hands over his groin. Still, I can think of half a dozen Alanis songs that, while not as bitter, are far more whacked than "You Oughta Know," especially those nutty tracks on which she chants in free verse over humming drones that sound like Tibetan bumblebees. *Om renge kyo*, already.

I attended an Alanis Morissette concert at the Greek Theater a few years ago and have to say, I came away wholly impressed, my only complaint being that it was too short. She sang great, played acoustic guitar, and was completely charming. Likewise her backup band was solid, playing imaginative new arrangements of her hits. She did "You Oughta Know," of course, and while it totally rocked, it was also her weakest song of the night. It's seemed as though she was singing it out of obligation, and that the emotional fury that lead her to write it originally had long dissipated. In more recent years Alanis has been a Chick with Aesthetic Introspection. Maybe she finally stopped dating those asshole guys who later got vivisected in her songs. Maybe all that yoga she's been doing has calmed her down. Maybe she's too rich to worry about it. She oughta know.

I'M NOT IN LOVE

Words and music by Eric Stewart and Graham Gouldman
Performed by 10cc
Released 1975
(No. 2 in U.S., No. 1 in UK; reissued 1995: No. 29 in UK)

```
AHHHHHHHHHHHHHHHHHHHHHHHHHHHHHHH
AHHHHHHHHHHHHHHHHHHHHHHHHHHHAAHHH
HHHHAHHAHHHHHHHHHAHHHAHHHHHHH
AHHHHHHAHHHHHAHHHHHHHHHHHHHHHH
HHHHHHHHHHHHHHAHHHHHHHHHHHHHHHH
HHHHHHHHAAHHHHHHHAHHAHHHHHHHH
HAHHHAHHHHHHHAHHHHHHAHHHHHHAHH
HHHHHHHHHHHHHHHHHHHHHHHHHHHAHH
HHHHHHHHHHHHHHHHHHHHHHAAHHHHHH
HAHHAHHHHHHHHHAHHHAHHHHHHHHAHH
HHHHAHHHHHAHHHHHHHHHHHHHHHHHHH
HHHHHHHHHHHAHHHHHHHHHHHHHHHHHH
HHHHHAAHHHHHHHAHHAHHHHHHHHHAH
HHAHHHHHHHAHHHHHHAHHHHH
```

THE PRECEDING blanket of nebulous white noise comes courtesy of a group who overdubbed their voices one hundred thousand times so that they could duplicate the sound of condemned souls moaning inside a darkened monastery while the monks were outside playing Frisbee. The idea was to layer it like a quarry full of dry ice over a haunted Fender Rhodes piano track and create one of the most mind-blowing creepy hit singles of the last millennium. This is how 10cc served up pop melodrama at its finest with "I'm Not in Love."

An offshoot of the pop group the Mindbenders, 10cc were part of the arty seventies English music scene along with Queen, Roxy

Music, Be Bop Deluxe, Electric Light Orchestra, and other groups who went schizoid in the studio trying to reinvent Beatles engineering. Their syringelike moniker was rumored to be from the amount of semen produced in a typical ejaculation (this probably isn't true but try it out as a topic of conversation). The group had a yin-yang dynamic in its four members, with Eric Stewart and Graham Gouldman being the pop single types while Lol Creme and Kevin Godley were the let's-see-what-this-button-does experimental types. A mainstay on the English charts for most of the 1970s, their lone crossover hit in the U.S. was the ultra-eerie "I'm Not in Love," which, its genius aside, was the one song you *did not* want to hear on the car radio while you were making out. Nothing froze the mood of pubescent canoodling worse than this bitter anthem of denial, especially when the bizarre whispering appeared in the middle of it (more on that in a bit).

The production of "I'm Not in Love" could only have happened in the seventies, when the painstaking overdubbing and layering of thousands of human voices didn't seem like a stupendous waste of time. As digital samplers didn't exist, the four members of 10cc sang and recorded every note of the chromatic scale in unison while overdubbing innumerable times, then went through a frenzy of mixing, looping, and processing to create the only choir to get a booking on the banks of the River Styx.

THE SONG

"I'm Not in Love" doesn't start like most songs. It's more like it appears, drifting in vaporously on a vamping electric piano while towing its choir of lost souls behind it like a kite.

Now imagine that you're huddled in the front seat of your car on a warm summer evening locking lips, trading tongues, and copping a feel with your crush of the week. The night wind blows gently through the trees and the radio is on low. (I know, most of you would have your iPod plugged into it, but just go with me on this, OK?) You're digging the rush of the first grope, the second base, the disheveled clothing. The whole scenario is teenage perfect when all of a sudden, *this* song comes on the radio.

"I'm not in love," some guy sings plaintively, telling the girl to not forget it. He insists that he's only going through a temporary phase so she shouldn't misunderstand his intentions just because he calls her. There's nothing going on with him because "I'm not in love" (the shortest chorus to a song ever written). Meanwhile, the choir "aaaaahhhhhhhhhs" over everything like tabernacle control freaks.

The mood in the car cools slightly. You two break off your tonsil probing and look at each other. You look at the radio. The guy ratchets up his denial in the second stanza, singing that he'd like to see her but then insisting it doesn't mean she means all that much to him. The awkwardness of the line sounds deliberate, the kind of redundant rationalization you'll hear . . . from each other in about a week. "Don't make a fuss" if he calls, he sings. And don't tell your friends about them either. ("Aaaaaaaaaaahhhhhhhhhhhhhhhhhhhhhhh.")

The instruments fade except for the choir. A pinging piano plays a melancholy phrase echoed by an ensemble of strings. As a Fender bass plays a sublime fill, the creepiest-sounding thing ever is heard. A hushed female voice appears in the song's middle like the ghost of a murdered girl. "Be quiet," she whispers. "Big boys don't cry, big boys don't cry, big boys don't cry . . ." Maybe not, but big boys get freaked, as do big girls. You both bolt upright, nervously asking, *why is there a ghost nymph coming out of my radio?* If you had the sense that nature gave a flea, you'd turn this mood-killing ballad off, but you can't. It's so captivating, so trancelike, all you can do is sit and feel your libido die off.

Finally the third stanza comes and the guy says how he keeps her picture on the wall because "it hides a nasty stain" that's under it. He also tells her he won't give it back to her so don't bother asking. The photo doesn't mean that much to him but she still can't have it. He's not in love . . .

("Aaaaaaaaaahhhhhhhhhhhhhhhhhhhhhhhh . . .") For his final lyric, he says how she'll have to wait a long time for him to be in love with her so she shouldn't hold her breath. ("Aaaaaaaaaahhhhhhhhhhhhhhhhhhhhhhhh . . .")

The song ends the same way it began, this time slowly disappearing in a veil of mist as the song's chorus rings in your head. Finally you snap out of it and turn off the radio. All you hear is the chirp of crickets. Neither of you feels like picking up where you left off. These arty-farty English guys and their damned nuclear choir just ruined the nookie ambience inside the car forever.

WHY IT'S CREEPY

"I'm Not in Love" is often misinterpreted as a kiss-off song when it's just the opposite. The lyrics are all about denial, where every claim of not caring rings hollow and it's obvious the guy's still angry about their breakup. It's a "thou doth protest too much" scenario you don't hear that often in a love song, especially one as avant-garde as this one. But while the lyrics are undeniably intense, the song's true creepiness comes from its extravagant airy production. I've listened to "I'm Not in Love" for over thirty years and it's never failed to creep me out while mesmerizing me all the same (I only recently noticed that there are no drums in it). Once you hear "I'm Not in Love" through a pair of quality headphones, you'll never listen to a vocal choir the same way again. It's an astounding song that still sounds fresh even today.

That said, you still don't want "I'm Not in Love" playing anywhere near you while you're in the throes of passion. Even if you can get past the aaahhh-ing voices and cloudy-with-chance-of-showers electric piano, you'll still want to crawl under the covers to hide from the whispering succubus ordering you not to cry. Who knows how many backseat rendevous were interrupted back when this song was in regular rotation on Top 40 radio?

ANGELS FUCK

Words and music by Jessika Fodera, Robin Moulder, Laura
Simpson-Kopsaftis, and R. Tucci
Performed by Jack Off Jill
Released 1997 (no chart position)

FOR THE most part, I had to find every creepy love song in this
book, both good and bad, on my own. People just weren't
forthcoming with lists or spontaneous suggestions like they were
for my previous depressing songs book. A few, like Phil Spector's
"To Know Him Is to Love Him," were recommended, but I was
already considering them anyway. It was rare for a song I'd never
heard of to drop whole cloth into my lap, lyrics and all, which
floored me enough to be considered a finalist. This was how the
wonderfully sick song "Angels Fuck" came to me.

As is required by United Nations mandate, I have a MySpace
page, and it was there I received a Friends request from a girl I'll
call Lana (not her real name). At the time of this writing, she was
a seventeen-year-old girl who, to make no small point of it,
wanted to kill herself. She expressed as much on her own
MySpace page, posting images of cutting, animated bloody
knives, and a scene from a movie where a character commits
suicide running in a loop. She had one older brother who'd died
from a drug overdose while another had his own drug problems.
Concerned, I e-mailed her and we began corresponding.

Along with my attempts to persuade her to continue counseling,
I told Lana about my creepy love songs book and asked if she had
any songs to suggest. A few days later she e-mailed me the lyrics to
nine songs, including "Whiskey Lullaby," which I was already
working on. Another one, though, was "Angels Fuck," which I'd
never heard of. I'd already endured a month's worth of CHAI

songs, with angels flitting in and out of half of them, so when a song entitled "Angels Fuck" showed up, my first thought was, well, I've *got to* hear this. Needless to say, I wasn't disappointed.

"Angels Fuck" is a song by Jack Off Jill, a four-piece band from Florida who had a long association with shock rocker Marilyn Manson, often touring as his opening act. This (mostly) all-female group scuffled about for eight years and released six albums before breaking up in 2000. I sampled their music and heard an anxious mélange of riot grrrl thrashing mixed with goth flourishes and punk snottiness. In other words, they never had a chance in hell of making it big. While I'm way too old to relate to their songs about cats, girl scouts, and various brown things, lead singer Jessika Fodera's voice was fantastic. She also scared the shit out of me, as evidenced in "Angels Fuck," still one of freakiest, creepiest things you'll ever hear—it ends with total emotional breakdown of Ms. Fodera that sounds so real, it just might be.

THE SONG

A tense punk guitar playing a descending interval opens "Angels Fuck," seemingly mimicking the downward slide of a depressed teenage mind. Jessika quietly sings of waking up in the morning feeling "dead today," having aged a "thousand years." She's having boyfriend problems and flinches every time he's nice to her. I can already see this guy, a skinny pierced doofus in a Godsmack shirt who cannot utter a single sentence without the word "dude" in it. He can kill her with a single word and when "angels fuck and devils kiss," she's sure about it. I admit I don't understand what angels fucking have to do with anything, but at least the angels are having some fun for once and not serving time in a Tori Amos song.

As the song continues, we see that there's a fissure in the adolescent relationship.

While she's willing to bask in his "forever," all he does is waste her time. This triggers her first break from reality as she sings how she wants to drag him down and end the world. Finally, she completely loses it when she declares herself "THAT SPECIAL GIRL!!!" The full caps don't do this justice. You simply must listen to the song to appreciate the frightening changeover that occurs here.

The band switches to a pounding punk beat as Jessika anxiously sings how everyone else has things to hide and people to crush but her. Her life is nothing but adolescent mediocrity and she can't trust anyone. During this chorus break, you can hear a strange cacophony of screaming layered in the background. I'm assuming it's the sound of angels fucking.

The disintegrating guitar intervals return and Jessika shares her scary scary dreams with us. She dreamed that "I was you" and that his ego died. She pities anyone who might love him more than she does because she knows he lied. She repeats how he's a waste of time. Meanwhile, "angels fuck and devils screw." Wow, all the celestial beings are getting in on this. Jessika's next breakdown is coming and it's going to be a big one. She wants to "piss in your heart" and become "THAT SPECIAL GIRL!!!"

In the pummeling chorus she repeats how everyone has things to hide and people to crush but her. But now she's gone off the edge and isn't coming back anytime soon, judging by the screaming maelstrom that erupts. She begins by singing "Hate you, love me, love me, hate you" before shrieking "Fuck you, fuck you, fuck me, fuck you" in a voice normally heard during exorcisms. There is an awful lot of obscene spewing heard at this point, yet Jessika somehow manages to make each one sound progressively more homicidal. (By the way, this is *in addition* to the screaming in the background.) Finally, just when you expect her lungs to collapse, the song ends with a somber piano playing us out while Jessika is heard (literally) pounding the floor screaming "IT WILL ALWAYS HURT, YOU FUCKING ASSHOLE!!" And that's a wrap.

WHY IT'S CREEPY

At first I didn't know what to make of "Angels Fuck." I guess one has to be an angry teenager in order to appreciate it, or at least a budding fan of schizophrenia. I'm not sure I would've included this song if it weren't for Jessika Fodera's near-brilliant performance. I've never heard anyone go from sweet angelic to shrieking psychotic as effortlessly as she does, like someone's meds wearing off in the time it takes to flip a light switch. Not even Axl Rose could conjure up so much bile so immediately— and especially not someone as petite and seemingly demure as Fodera. She's ten times the singer Courtney Love is and far more interesting. I had to pull my socks up after listening to "Angels Fuck," immediately concluding that it's one of the creepiest things I've heard.

That said, is it a quality song? Probably not, but it's so damned nuts you don't care. Lately I've been opening my ears to music I'd previously avoided and finding I enjoy it more than I thought I would. I'd rather listen to Jack Off Jill's offbeat crashings than L7's tedious riot grrrl shtick. But while I appreciate the artistic impulse that drives the genre, I've always felt the punk/goth/alternative music scene is somewhat delusional. Curse me ye may but the truth is *nobody buys this stuff.* Sure, eighty-odd people may cram into a room designed to hold fifty to watch six bands perform, and a thousand people will show up to see a Sleater-Kinney farewell concert, but that does not a movement make. The big musical movement is called *American Idol.* Deal with it.

As for Lana, we're still in touch and she has her good days and bad days. When she turns eighteen, she hopes to move out, get her own place, and attend a vocational school. She has her GED and wants to get into graphic arts. While we've never spoken except via e-mail, I think I hear a little of Lana's voice during the bitter climax to "Angels Fuck," except she's screaming at things way beyond an errant boyfriend. She's screaming "fuck you" at life. Although that's not the best way to live, it'll have to do for now. It's better than giving up.

ALL IN THE FAMILY

ALIVE

Words and music by Eddie Vedder and Stone Gossard
Performed by Pearl Jam
Released 1991 (No. 16 on U.S. rock charts, No. 16 in UK)

WHEN PEARL Jam first exploded in the early nineties, the group came with the grunge tag, as if distortion and flannel were some radical new discoveries. I've always considered Pearl Jam a broken jaw band, because I'll be damned if I could understand what anyone was saying.

If you think I'm a heretic, do this: listen to the songs "Animal" and "Black," then tell me what the lyrics are to either one *without looking them up first*. You can't. Even the guy who broke the Germans' Enigma code during the Second World War couldn't figure them out. (You, reader, the one who used to be music director at your college radio station, I can see you bristling at what I wrote. Fine, I'll qualify it. Nobody understands the lyrics except *you*.) This is significant because the garbled song "Alive" broke Pearl Jam into the mainstream and helped push their debut album *Ten* to platinum status, leading to a *Time* magazine cover, massive CD sales, and sellout stadium tours. Great. "Alive" is about incest, but yeah, great.

"Alive" is supposedly part of something called the "Mamasan Trilogy," consisting of three songs cowritten by Vedder that have nothing to do with each other than that they're all sorta creepy. According to Vedder, "Alive" is inspired by his own experience as a boy when he discovered the man he thought was his father was actually his stepfather (his birth father had died years earlier). This scenario could've been interesting for a song, but Vedder put an Oedipal twist on it by making the boy in "Alive" become the, ahem, *recipient* of his mother's affection. Most listeners didn't know this, although they did fall in love with the chorus in which the phrase "I'm still alive" gets Vedder-ized into "Ohhhh Iiii-aye, whoaaaa-ohhh, ahm stulllll ahh-laaavvve, ohhh-ayyyy . . ."

THE SONG

"Alive" almost didn't make the book as a few people, including my editor, recommended Pearl Jam's "Black" for a creepy love song. I tried it out and heard this for the first verse: "Sheeeee aaaaa ehhhhh-eeeee caaaaa-ehssss." For the record, that's "Sheets of empty canvas." Eddie Vedder is the only man I know who's afraid of consonants.

So I returned to "Alive," the first Pearl Jam song I'd ever heard. Everything about it is textbook grunge, including the slurring fuzzy guitars, plodding tempo, and Novocain vocals, along with a foreshadowing of the ultraseriousness that helped kill grunge a few years later. The song begins with a fuzzbox guitar playing a strained riff as though it's pulling taffy out of a dryer's lint trap. The band drops in to set up a sludgelike groove while Vedder places us in a teenage boy's bedroom with his mother. "Saaaan, she sehh-d, haah I gah-a l'l stoa-y faa' yuuu . . ." (she wants to tell him something). "Whhaa y' thaw wah yo 'addy wah n'thn . . ." (it's about his father). She goes on to say how when he was "'irteen," his real father passed away and it's too bad he never met him, "but ahm glai-d we 'awked" (she's happy she told him).

On to the chorus! "Ohhhh Iiii-aye, whoaaaa-ohhh, ahm stulllll ahh-laaavvve, ohhh-ayyyy . . ."

So to recap, a teenage boy has learned that his real father is dead but his mother certainly isn't. She's the one telling him she's still "ahh-laaavvve." Now things take a creepy turn. Ooh creepy creepy. Mom begins to sashay across the "yawng man' rheumm," posing next to the bong and Mother Love Bone poster. "Ahm rea'y f'r yuuu," she tells him. "What'd you say?" he asks. "I said, ahm rea'y f'r yuuu!" she snaps (she's ready for him to sleep with her). At this point, the boy doesn't remember what happens next save "th' loo', th' loo'" on her face. "Naw ahh can' seeee . . ."

The chorus, the chorus! "Ohhhh Iiii-aye, whoaaaa-ohh, ahm stulllll ahh-laaavvve, ohhh-ayyyy . . ."

The music settles into a tepid jangle during the bridge. Mom notices her son's reluctant expression. "S' s'mthi' wraawng?" she asks him. "Wel' co-rs' the-r iis . . ." he says, adopting Mom's syntax. Mom reminds him how she's ahh-laaavvve, he's ahh-laaavvve, they're both ahh-laaavvve. The kid asks if he deserves to be ahh-laaavvve. We're left with this question while wondering "whoo ann-sahs, whoo ann-sahs . . ."

And-a one, and-a two. "Ohhhh Iiii-aye, whoaaaa-ohh . . ."

The song builds to a lethargic jam while featuring a guitar solo that is curiously listed as one of the hundred best guitar solos of all time by *Guitar* magazine. I don't know why as it's the same sort of pentatonic noodling played every night by a thousand different bands paying to perform in a thousand different clubs. The presence of a floppy wah-wah pedal doesn't help matters much. Finally it crashes to a conclusion just as the last stage diver gets dropped to the pavement.

WHY IT'S CREEPY

Since its 1991 release, I estimate I'd heard "Alive" around 23,891 times while only deciphering that a mother was in her son's room trying to accomplish something. I finally ran out of patience and Googled the freaking lyrics. Now I've figured out the rest and realized "Alive" is even creepier than I assumed it was, and not in a good way. Like the other two songs of the so-called Mamasan Trilogy, "Once" and "Footsteps," "Alive" exemplifies the pretentious and self-important excesses that befell grunge groups and turned them into boring wank fests. Listening to bands like Mudhoney having anxiety attacks over "selling out" and "artistic integrity" while impaling themselves to get record contracts really got tiresome. As for Eddie Vedder and Pearl Jam, they greeted every platinum sale of their CDs as some kind of whore deal, and by 1994 I was ready to scream "Shut the hell up already" when Kurt Cobain martyred himself with a twenty-gauge.

While the decline of grunge is attributed to Cobain's suicide and overbearing media attention, I think the 1996 music documentary *Hype!* shows what was really behind its collapse. A smartly produced chronicle of the nineties' Seattle grunge phenomenon, the film features more than thirty bands in performance. The problem is, twenty-six of them suck. They couldn't play, couldn't write, and couldn't perform. Most sounded like sixteen-year-olds pretending to be Neil Young's Crazy Horse. The best moment in the whole film is an electrifying debut performance of "Smells Like Teen Spirit" by a then-unknown Nirvana, shot inside a seedy club. Sure, Cobain was not exactly a diction freak, but the band's raw sound was fresh and original, eclipsing practically every one of its contemporaries. Pearl Jam has good musicians, but I've found Vedder to be a tedious vocalist who takes himself way too seriously. But at least the band is still "ahhh-laavve."

ME AND MY OLD LADY

Words and music by Dexter Holland
Performed by the Offspring
Released 1996 (no chart position)

DIRECTLY BELOW the greater Los Angeles area is the sprawling enclave of Orange County. For years, nobody had ever heard of it. Even residents of Orange County didn't know they lived in Orange County. They only knew they lived in Anaheim, Brea, Fullerton, Costa Mesa, Tustin, Mission Viejo, Laguna Beach, Irvine, or any of a dozen other cities. It wasn't until snotty punk bands began popping up during the 1980s that the Orange County label came to prominence because it was simpler to promote. Recently it's been shortened to just O.C. Eventually it'll be called "Oc" (pronounced *ahk*) and all of its cities will meld together into one big metropolis called Not Los Angeles.

The O.C. punk music scene was different from L.A.'s in that the bands were richer and had better tans. They didn't live in the kind of squalor the L.A. punks did, as seen in the excellent 1981 documentary *The Decline of Western Civilization*. O.C. punk bands tended to be technically superior, too, because they could afford better equipment and guitars that stayed in tune. They also sold way more albums because they were savvy enough to stop playing traditional punk and instead mixed in power pop, metal, and glam rock with their songs. One of the most successful of these bands is the Offspring.

The Offspring is a four-piece band formed in 1984 by Bryan "Dexter" Holland, an Orange County native who holds a Masters degree in molecular biology (as punk band members usually do). The band's 1994 album *Smash* was indeed a smash, selling six million copies, with other O.C. groups like Lit and No

Doubt following in their wake. The Offspring's songs are mostly tongue-in-pierced-cheek, centering on losers, goofballs, and stoners living in a perpetual state of ennui while an angry girlfriend yells at them, i.e. "Self-Esteem," "Why Don't You Get a Job," "The Kids Aren't Alright," etc. Since few Offspring tracks should be taken seriously, I won't be scrutinizing their song "Me and My Old Lady" as though it's a newly discovered Platonic dialogue. All I know is that it's loud, unwashed, and creepy.

THE SONG

"She ain't no ball and chain! She ain't no ball and chain!" This is how "Me and My Old Lady" begins, with full punk a capella snottiness. A pair of speedball guitars built out of old skateboard ramps tears out jagged slanted riffs that sound vaguely oriental. "Me and my old lady," vocalist Holland screams, "lay in bed all day" (it should be "lie in bed," but how punk would that be?). Uh-oh, this isn't good, another damned song about nothing. Even when the guy says he loves her it causes her to roll away from him. No Jewel-like relationship conversations happening anytime soon. However, he will concede that if he believes in love then "there's nothing wrong with my head."

This song's premise is simple: a white trash couple crashes on a soiled mattress from dawn till dusk trying to think of new ways to be inert. Who this couple is, however, is a different story. Is it a thirty-year-old slacker who works at a video shop in bed with his ragamuffin nineteen-year-old girlfriend? Or is it a thirty-year-old slacker who works at a video shop in bed with his forty-eight-year-old mother? Either way, they're about three crystal meth hits away from being featured on the next episode of *Cops*. "Me and my old lady," Holland continues, "sit and sip on wine." He fails to mention it's ten in the morning, the wine's label says ". . . and other fruit flavors," and the landlord's pounding on the door demanding the rent. Now it's the old lady's turn. "She says she loves me," sings Holland, forcing him to tell her that "love is blind." Still, like him, if she believes in love then her head's OK too. So at least they've got that in common, that and chlamydia.

The fastest transition to a bridge in the history of music occurs, and now everyone's acting all defiant. They're both making a scene, and she doesn't care who hears them. It's not as though anyone's going to call and complain; the phone's disconnected anyway. She's groping him, grabbing him, smothering him with kisses from her fever-blistered lips. "We ain't gonna change," Holland sings defiantly. Go ahead and stare at them because they don't care.

So far nothing much has happened in this song other than the carnal grappling of two mobile home troglodytes whose dream is a guest shot on *Jerry Springer*. But are they son and mother? The term "old lady" is interchangeable slang nowadays and it's dated too. I'm more grossed out at the thought of these unwashed future blood transfusion recipients pressing their stinky naked bodies together so much that it sounds like Velcro separating when he rolls off of her.

"Me and my old lady," Holland wails, "suck each other dry." Please let his be a vampire reference; otherwise I don't want to know. He insists that he's a lucky man and that they'll continue passing the day "quenching our libidos" while ignoring the landlord's angry knocking, the turned-off electricity and the cockroaches the size of Cuban cigars crawling on the wall. "She ain't no ball and chain!"

WHY IT'S CREEPY

Of the numerous incest songs I've endured over the last several months, "Me and My Old Lady" is the chirpiest. There's a lot of strange optimism to it, and the couple definitely love each other in their own venereal way. Maybe it's not about incest and is simply a joyous anthem to love in the trailer park. Is it really going to make these two any less revolting? You can still pretty much smell this denizen couple along with their stained mattress, crusty linens, and pizza boxes strewn around them. I'm all for couples spending a romantic day in bed together, but not two unemployed slack-jawed cretins who need penicillin even more than they need career counseling. The fact that the Offspring, not Sinatra, are singing about them means they've already hocked their skateboards to buy some weed and a DVD copy of *Idle Hands*. The only thing left is for them to pass out with lit cigarettes in their hands and end up getting scorched like Roman candles.

Now let's consider the other scenario: these two are gross, stupid, stoned, broke, dirty, unemployed, having dual herpes outbreaks, *and* they're mother and son. On second thought, let's not.

FATHER FIGURE

Words and music by George Michael
Performed by George Michael
Released 1988 (No. 1 in U.S., No. 11 in UK)

WHEN GEORGE Michael was arrested in 1998 for "engaging in a lewd act," I just assumed he'd been collaborating with Madonna. When I found out the lewd act was an incident involving a male undercover officer inside a public bathroom in Beverly Hills, I have to say I was completely shocked. I didn't know Beverly Hills allowed public bathrooms.

When he began his career as one half of the teen idol duo Wham! George Michael always managed to circumvent any label that might compromise his career. Before critics had a chance to nail him for the bubble-gummy "Wake Me Up (Before You Go-Go)," he returned with "Careless Whisper" and other hits before bolting from Wham! to pursue a solo career. For years he played the unshaven rogue bit with his aviator sunglasses and leather jacket while featuring lingerie-clad sirens surrendering to his every whisker burn in racy music videos. Meanwhile, the public was noticing how distracted he looked while stroking a woman's bare thigh.

After Michael came out as gay, confirmed by researchers at Duh, Inc., it lent an interesting twist on all those videos while changing the context of his songs. "Faith" and "Careless Whisper" may work fine, but something like "I Want Your Sex," with all its lusting appeals for female flesh, sounds a little strange. But if any song stayed as creepy as it ever was, it was "Father Figure," one of the four No. 1 songs from his 1987 album *Faith*. I never understood why people didn't react to it more, because if you listen to the song's lyrics, it has a Lolita theme that's too obvious to ignore.

THE SONG

The musical track to "Father Figure" is another eighties analog synthesizer showcase, with fluffy ethereal chords blanketing the entire track. As the Roland keyboard lays its topcoat, George sings how all he wants is something special, which is to be "bold and naked at your side." Who he's addressing is never specified, so I'll let you, the reader, fill that in. If you prefer the closeted George, he's seducing Linda Evangelista. If you want the George of today, he's bedding the drummer from Culture Club. Sometimes he thinks that he'll never be understood, adding that she (he) wants the same thing as he does, namely for someone to be warm and naked by her (his) side, too. Together, they'd be happy.

This is all fine up to here. It's the chorus that takes everything down Creep Alley. "I will be your Father Figure," Michael sings, telling him (her) to put "your tiny hand" in his. He offers to be "your preacher teacher" and "your daddy," while adding he's had "enough of crime." At this point, it doesn't matter who he's addressing; wouldn't anyone feel a little queasy if someone made an overture like this?

If you think I'm reading too much into this, consider the next stanza, where George sings how love can sometimes be "mistaken for a crime." That's the second crime reference in so many bars of synth wash. What exactly are he and his father fraternity up to anyway? "If we have faith," he sings, then they can be strong. The chorus appears again and George repeats his offer to be the Father Figure, preacher teacher, one half of Wham! whatever you may have in mind.

OK, there's something odd going on here. It seems George Michael is setting up a relationship with someone who needs an allowance and to be in bed by ten. I'm sure everyone involved is a consenting adult, but does the other person really want to call him Father George? During the bridge, George loses inspiration and throws out tired references to her (him) being the "desert" while he's the "sea," proving that America's "Horse with No Name" is still being played on the radio. But when he returns to the verse section George tips his hand again by whispering, "Greet me with the eyes of a child." The choir-laden chorus appears one last time and all the preacher/father/daddy declarations come tumbling out via an anxious set of concluding verses. The synth pads and sublime percussion fade into the eighties atmosphere.

WHY IT'S CREEPY

For a hit single, "Father Figure" is pretty long, almost six minutes. But then again, maybe you need time to establish a paternal-like control over your new main squeeze, which is what George Michael seems to do in this song. "Father Figure" defies the romantic ballad genre because it has way too many call-me-daddy references to be a coincidence, and therein lies its creepiness. I'm not such a bastard as to suggest that he's making a play for a minor, because he's never even been rumored to be that way. No, it's a full-grown adult that he's courting in "Father Figure," one with tiny hands, tiny feet, and if we believe the myth, a tiny, tiny soldier. Or maybe it's one of the 428 models in the *Freedom 90* video and he's trying to be her ubiquitous gay best friend. Personally, I'd prefer it be the former because there's nothing more annoying than dating a girl who's got a chatty uber-witty gay pal who she drags everywhere with her like a Streisand-loving poodle.

George Michael did a lot of sexually suggestive songs during his *Faith* period and after, including the graphic "I Want Your Sex," that in hindsight seemed like an anxious attempt to dispel gay rumors about him that hadn't even started yet. Maybe "Father Figure" was written for the same reason. Maybe he was just singing from a character's point of view. Or maybe his life partner has to ask permission to borrow the car keys.

MY HEART BELONGS TO DADDY

Words and music by Cole Porter
Performed by Julie London
Released 1956 (No. 13 in U.S.)

THE HISTORY of popular culture is rife with controversies that, years later, compel the next generation to wonder what all the fuss was about. Although he was hounded into near-ruin for violating obscenity laws, the routines of comedian Lenny Bruce today seem harmless (they're more striking now for how strange they sound, like a bebop sax solo in the middle of a Foo Fighters song). It's rare for something to be more startling later on than when it first appeared, but when it happens, it's a hell of a lot of fun. There is no better example of this than the sick-ass Cole Porter song "My Heart Belongs to Daddy."

Although he's all but forgotten today, Cole Porter was one of the most famous American songwriters of the twentieth century, a flamboyant gay bon vivant who lived much of his life in agonizing pain after being badly injured in a horse-riding accident. Porter was known for his suggestive songs like "Too Darn Hot," as well as for romantic love ballads like the haunting "Night and Day." It was a challenge for me to find which version of "My Heart Belongs to Daddy" to consider, as hundreds of performers have recorded it. So rather than find a "camp" version by somebody butchering it with drag queen conceit, I zeroed in on Julie London, whose 1956 rendition of "My Heart Belongs to Daddy" is both creepy and fantastic.

It's likely that readers have never heard of Julie London, a vastly underrated singer whose voice oozed so much sex appeal that she could make "The Star-Spangled Banner" sound like a mash note. Working as both an actress and vocalist, Ms. London scored several hit records in the mid-1950s, starting with a seductive cover of "Cry Me a River." A stunning woman, she was notorious for her album covers that featured her lounging seductively in tight, form-fitting gowns (she later joked that they spent more time designing her albums than producing her songs). Critics at the time unfairly dismissed London as an undistinguished vocalist, and she never took herself seriously, modestly downplaying her skills as a singer. She went on to live a scandal-free life, raising children and being a devoted wife to her husband, the talented songwriter Bobby Troup ("Route 66"), before her death in 2000 at the age of seventy-four. In recent years, new legions of fans have discovered her smoky singing and sexually tinged interpretations of love songs that flew right past audiences of the time (very little of her recorded work sounds dated today).

THE SONG

"My Heart Belongs to Daddy" first appeared in the terrible 1938 musical *Leave It to Me*, for which Porter wrote the music and lyrics. Back then, hit songs often originated from Broadway productions, so "My Heart Belongs to Daddy" was part of *Leave It to Me*'s idiotic storyline (a homesick U.S. ambassador to Russia tries to sabotage his own career so he can be fired and get sent back to his hometown of Topeka, Kansas. I'm not making this up). In the following years, various performers covered the song, but it took the sultry magic of Julie London to give it the vaguely incestuous overtones its title suggests.

London's recording begins with a solo walking bass while a Tinkerbell-like chime drops accents on every other bar. Then her voice, mixed WAY UP FRONT, enters: she casually admits to making advances towards the caddy while "tearing off" a game of golf. However, it becomes clear she's just a big tease, because she never follows through. Her heart, mind, and soul "belong to Daddy," ba-da-BOP! (horn accents; listen to the song, it'll make sense). Next, the kinky Ms. London enjoys inviting a boy over for "some fine finnan haddie," supposedly a term for Scottish haddock and one of the most contrived setups for a rhyme ever conceived. The guest inevitably begs for more but, sorry, her heart belongs to Daddy, ba-da-BOP (horn stab again; it's catchy).

The chorus repeats her love for Da-Da as a bed of syrupy strings plays behind her. It's here where you wonder who in the world is she singing about. Who exactly is "Daddy" and why does her heart belong to him? "I simply couldn't be bad," she insists. Yes, your groping dad may not approve. She warns us that, while she knows we're perfectly swell, her heart will always belong to Daddy because he treats her so darn well.

After a brief swinging interlude of horns and rhythm section, London repeats the verses from the top. She's grabbing the crotch of yet another caddy but, uh-uh, that's all he gets because Daddy gets the rest. Meanwhile, another horny boy gets invited over and he pleads to be allowed inside the Tower of London. Instead she shows him the door because Daddy's waiting upstairs. Her heart will always belong to him. Ba-da-BOP!

WHY IT'S CREEPY

If they're not already dead, there are probably a few Cole Porter aficionados who take umbrage with my incestuous interpretation of this song. Well, he started it. How else does one decipher a song where the singer is dedicating her heart to Daddy? More importantly, would anyone write a number like this today and not expect people to think there's something a little unsavory going on? While I haven't seen *Leave It to Me* (which will never be revived), I'm guessing the song has a different meaning to it within the book's storyline. Fine, whatever; all I know is that it always draws snickers from audience members whenever a cabaret vocalist pulls it out of the trunk.

London's version of the song is pretty short in duration, lasting less than three minutes, which is yet another refreshing aspect of her catalog. Her recordings were usually brief and she could knock off half a dozen in one day without even thinking about it (she released thirty-two albums in less than ten years). It's this relaxed approach combined with her effortless, sexy vocals that make her songs float along like libidinous moths without a hint of pretense. She phrased easily with a light touch during up-tempo numbers, yet could be devastating on ballads; her recording of "My Funny Valentine" is one of the most erotic performances ever.

Many people's final exposure to Julie London was in the 1970s TV series *Emergency*, in which she played Nurse Dixie McCall. Pushing fifty at the time, she was ridiculously miscast, yet her silvery hair, sleepy eyes, and martini-accented voice made her irresistible, the first grand-MILF. Even when the camera caught her at a bad angle and aged her four score and seven years, she was still a pro who knew both her strengths and her limitations. Whoever you are, throw away your Rod Stewart standards CD and give Julie London a try. You might end up getting laid.

INCESTUOUS LOVE
(AMOURS INCESTUEUSES)

Original French lyrics and music by Barbara (Monique Serf)
English-language version performed by Marc Almond
Released 1996 (no chart position)

"INCESTUOUS LOVE" is the weirdest song I've ever heard.

I've blinked to a German corpse love ballad (see "Marry Me"), gone mute from hearing "Fergalicious," and taken numerous showers to wash away the fetid stench of "I've Never Been to Me." But let me say it again: "Incestuous Love" is the weirdest song I've ever heard.

Is it the schizoid cabaret music? The heartrending lyrics? The fact that I spent three days tracking it down and the only version I could find is from the guy who used to be in Soft Cell? Whatever; my head's still reeling. I can't decide if this song is a touching ballad about a mother's love for her son or an egregious pile of inbred sickness.

First, some background: "Incestuous Love" began life as "Amours Incestueuses," written by the French cabaret artist Monique Serf, who performed under the stage name Barbara. Serf was born in 1930 and grew up to be a popular singer in the cabarets and music halls of France, eventually becoming a young contemporary of the celebrated Edith Piaf. She was known for her haunting voice and all-black hair and wardrobe, a Gallic goth as it were. She was also a prolific songwriter and composed many turbulent songs about lost love, found love, dead love, wounded love, slightly injured love, and even incestuous love, as evidenced by "Amours Incestueuses." An active performer throughout most of her life, Serf died in 1997 of respiratory failure.

As for the English-language version of "Incestuous Love," it appears on Marc Almond's 1996 album *Absinthe*. Before going solo, Almond was one-half of the English synthpop duo Soft Cell, so named because listening to their music softened brain cells. The group scored a No. 1 hit internationally in 1981 with their robotic version of the sixties Gloria Jones single "Tainted Love." You may remember Soft Cell's version for the *blonk blonk* stabs heard throughout the song that sound like a horn on a clown car. Almond went on to work as a solo artist, DJ, and producer while pursuing his interest in European cabaret-style music. His *Absinthe* album consists of English-language covers of French cabaret songs by Jacques Brel and Julliete Greco, and of course, Barbara's "Incestuous Love."

THE SONG

A series of dark-toned piano arpeggios plays gently while Almond sings in a rich poignant tenor from the perspective of a mother saying goodbye to her son, a "king, my child who I adore." The boy is her setting sun and if she should fall to the ground, "you are my final spring." She loves him dearly. But the mother is older now, having made her way into her autumn years. But the one miracle in her life was the boy who became king, who broke frontiers for her and became her sky, her ground. For all his years, he gave her his heart and became her final spring. If you haven't choked up, I'm not doing the song justice. At first I was floored while listening to Almond, his sentimentality totally in sync with the song. I thought I'd found an unknown gem. But then the gem turned an odd color.

The music breaks into a strange drunken waltz straight out of *Cabaret*. "I always thought," Almond sings with Weimar relish, the love that's beautiful is the one that's "incestuous." She sees it in his eyes, that he wants the two of them to live "the most beautiful love." Where the hell did this come from? Are mother and son married? Why does the music sound like the Reichstag caught fire last month? Right when I was surrendering to the beauty of the song, this craziness doth step forward hence. We hear that he's her "adolescent," her heartache who "laid your twenty years" with her "forty." Good Lord, she even kisses his mouth. She declares their love is a diamond they were both given and it became the "most beautiful love," an incestuous love. OK, I demand to know what's going on. Is this a French thing? I know we Americans are vulgar brutes who ruined their wine industry, but we're not so base that we can't see there's something terribly wrong here.

Almond stays with the oom-pah-pah music while singing of diamonds and burning cathedrals, which apparently symbolize the marvels of incestuous love. I always thought it was therapy and medication but OK, whatever. "Goodbye, my child," Almond sings. The mother hopes that one day the boy will understand how love also comes with loss, and she now must leave him as she conceals her pain. "My love, my child, my king, I love you." This is the truth from the depths of her heart.

WHY IT'S CREEPY

So here's what we have: a song in which much of the music is beautiful, the lyrics are filled with warmth and imagery, and Almond's performance is a marvel. Let's see, what else? Oh, yes, the mother is *having sex with her son*. What's odd is how earnest and organic it all seems within the context of the lyrics. So the creepiness is heightened by how incest is seen as something pure, something natural, or as the lyrics say, "the most beautiful love." The Brown Shirts waltz bit in the middle just makes it more twisted.

Although "Incestuous Love" is one of many songs I've heard that address incest, it remains the only French one. The French must be darn serious about their perversions, because they don't seem to have nearly the guilt, shame, and irony the rest of us do about our peccadilloes. There is an air of sophistication to

"Incestuous Love" that makes it too stylish and mature to be dismissed as either exploitive trash or a horrifically bad idea (see "Don't Stop Swaying"). Maybe it's an inaccurate translation. It wouldn't be the first time a work in a foreign language was transcribed into something gross in English. Perhaps the incest isn't physical but rather a spiritual karmic thing, one of those Zen garden chakra centering rituals that mothers can do to stay connected to their sons. Or maybe this Amours Incestueuses stuff is unique to the French, ah *oui, oui*. Is this why a Boy Scout troop could invade and take Paris within a week? All I know is that "Incestuous Love" is still the weirdest song I've ever heard.

DEATH BECOMES US

TO KNOW HIM IS TO LOVE HIM

Words and music by Phil Spector
Performed by the Teddy Bears
Released 1958 (No. 1 in U.S., No. 2 in UK)

I'D LIKE to tell you about my neighbor Art, the former manager of the eighties roots-rock band the Blasters. Art's the kind of guy who'd order Justin Timberlake to get off his lawn but would donate a kidney to anybody who played with Roy Orbison. He insists rock 'n' roll died forever in 1959; in fact, he swears to it. If you look up the word "purist" in the dictionary, you'll see a picture of Art standing next to Buddy Holly's crashed plane. Art also knows a lot of musicians who have been left by the wayside over the years; aging session players, rockabilly masters, the guy who wrote "My Sharona," etc. One day a few years ago, Art told me something you don't hear very often:

"I go bowling with Phil Spector."

"How does that work?" I asked.

"It's Phil's Monday Night Bowling Party," he said. "I go bowling with him and some guys who were with the Wrecking Crew.* It's a lot of fun."

Needless to say, it's been many years since Art has hit the lanes with Spector. Yet who among us wouldn't love to crash that party, just for a chance to see an elfin nut in a bad wig throwing a 7-10 split? I'm wondering if he shot at the remaining pins to get a spare. After all, Spector is what you call "colorful." (Tortured artists always have euphemisms flying around them. Let's stop wasting time and admit they're out of their fucking minds.) As I write this the batty Spector is awaiting a second trial

---

* The Wrecking Crew were legendary L.A. session musicians who played on scores of hit records during the 1960s and 1970s.

for the murder of B-movie actress Lana Clarkson, who was found shot to death inside his Los Angeles–area mansion in February 2003. The first trial ended in a hung jury of ten to two in favor of guilty.

Today's music fans know little about Spector, whose influence on pop music was immeasurable. A masterful arranger, he revolutionized the recording industry in the 1960s, utilizing his massive Wall of Sound production technique on dozens of hit songs for other artists. He was also crazy in that he pulled guns on people he worked with like the Ramones, ex-wife Ronnie Spector, and John Lennon (I'm aware of the latter's portent).

Spector's notoriously erratic personality is why his early hit "To Know Him Is to Love Him" is so much creepier now than it was when it was released in 1958. Spector wrote the song when he was only seventeen, borrowing the title from his father's tombstone. He and his first group, the Teddy Bears, recorded it in a cramped Hollywood studio in a few hours with a budget of a whopping $75. The song shot to No. 1 and stayed there for a month, giving Spector his entry into the music business.

THE SONG

It's time now for my annual Pachelbel joke. There's a long-running conspiracy theory that 75 percent of the pop ballads from the past fifty years were written using Pachelbel's Canon in D. Although it has its own sophistications, "To Know Him" contains enough baroque-era chord changes to make it Spector's Cannon in D. (A cannon's a gun. Get it?) What makes it unique is the creepy desperation in the lyrics that was missed by record buyers of the time.

After a brief intro, lead vocalist Annette Kleinbard sings of her love for someone called Him. Who Him might be is a mystery, possibly Steve the prom king, Bill the star quarterback, or Phil the unstable songwriter with the 9mm in his pocket. She sings that to know know know him is the best way to love love love him. A smile from Him makes her life worthwhile. When your ability to stay alive rests on somebody's facial expression, it's time to change homerooms.

She pledges that she'll be good to Him while offering love in the form of heavy reverb, mono sound mixes, and a fully loaded clip. Soon the day will come when she'll "walk alongside" Him because everybody tells her she will. They also tell her the dress she's wearing doesn't make her look fat. Now comes the best and creepiest part of the song, a bridge with an extraordinary set of chord substitutions that send the melody flying into bipolar territory. This is where we discover that our smitten singer is in love with someone who's unaware she exists. I don't mean outside-our-clique unaware, I mean did-you-hear-something-why's-it-so-cold-in-this-room unaware, the kind of existence requiring a psychic who's fluent in ectoplasm. "Why can't he see me?" she desperately sings, asking how blind is he anyway. She's hopeful that someday he'll realize that they were meant for each other. But first he'll have to pass through to the Other Side.

The song concludes with a repeat of the opening chorus before fading as if the meter just ran out on the studio time. "To know know know him . . ." Sorry sorry sorry but you're scaring the crap crap crap out of me.

WHY IT'S CREEPY

The unrequited love theme of the song is more sad when you consider how far off his radar this girl is. You just know she follows him around the halls of their school like a tethered balloon while keeping close to the lockers, her braces the size of a fence and acne resembling a satellite shot of Mars. Oh yeah—she's also dead. The poor girl is like every kid who died prematurely at my own high school. They always had a blurry photo of him on page 43 of the yearbook. The rest of us would gaze at it in silence before asking each other, "Who the hell was this guy?"

I will say that "To Know Him" holds up much better than most of those fifties white-girl prom ballads that sounded like a fifth-grader practicing arpeggios on the family spinet. Spector's music is very mature for a seventeen-year-old and the bridge is a harmonic marvel. The crude engineering only adds to the song's strange charm, while the heavy reverb gives it an ethereal sound. Linda Ronstadt, Dolly Parton, and Emmylou Harris together did a fine country remake of the song in 1987, but it doesn't quite match the tragic subtext of the original.

What ups the creepy factor of "To Know Him" today is Phil Spector's connection to it. Remember, this guy shot up John Lennon's studio. Try to imagine singing this song to Spector while being aware that to know know know him is to run run run from him. Without his involvement the song would probably be an obscure footnote in the story of rock 'n' roll. Instead, it's a bitter ode to a talented genius whose entire reputation has been laid to waste.

THERE IS A LIGHT THAT NEVER GOES OUT

Words and music by Morrissey and Johnny Marr
Performed by the Smiths
Released 1986 (No. 25 in UK)
Performed by Morrissey
Released 2005 (No. 11 in UK)

A CONFESSION: I never heard a single Smiths song while they were together. You heard me, not one. I'm from Wisconsin, and the group was from Manchester, UK. How was that gonna work? It's not as though Morrissey and company ever played the Marathon County Fair, sharing a stage with the Nitty Gritty Dirt Band. Was our local FM station going to forsake playing the Cars and Pat Benatar for "Heaven Knows I'm Miserable Now?" Not bloody likely (or as we Yanks say, hell, no). So I spent the eighties completely oblivious of the Smiths save for "How Soon Is Now," which I heard long after they broke up but didn't know who sang it because stations only played it once every thirteen months.

It was two decades later while researching depressing songs for my last book that I took a serious listen to the group's entire catalog. I came away impressed with Johnny Marr's rich guitar playing and convinced that Morrissey had created one of the most incongruous images for himself: a rock star who can't get laid. While I was prevented from including a Smiths song in the previous volume, I now have free rein to do so here. Besides, the group had almost as many creepy love songs as they did depressing ones.

I worked my way through the Smiths catalog again, revisiting

Marr's shimmering chords and Morrissey's mournful bleakness. (What's up with Manchester? Why's everybody so depressed there?) It was tough to select one, what with all the sexual neuroses and comatose girlfriends brightening up every other track. Even when Marr's music was pop and allegro, Morrissey could never see the sun shine. So when I came across "There's a Light That Never Goes Out," I knew it was the one. The song was creepy, depressing, and up-tempo, which meant it would be the second time I settled on a Smiths tune that wasn't a gloomy ballad. ("Miserable Lie" was my choice for the last book.) Plus, "There's a Light" has a proud anthemic edge to it with none of the Freudian confusion of "Cemetery Gates" or "Pretty Girls Make Graves."

THE SONG

"There's a Light" begins with jangly guitars playing minor chords while Morrissey tells the annoying American journalist at the session it's not an REM cover. (Before everyone gets pissy with me, play this song and almost anything from REM's first three albums. The similarity is striking at times and it's clear both bands were exploring comparable musical forms, albeit independently.) Morrissey sings of riding around in someone's car, although whom he's with is never specified. He writes so often in the first person, you're always unsure whom he's hanging out with.

"Take me home tonight," he sings in his melancholy voice. It's not his own home that he wants to go to; it's the driver's. Morrissey needs music and people who are young and alive like him. He doesn't want to go back to his own home because he doesn't have one any more.

Has he been thrown out? Is he an errant teenage lad whose parents have banished him from their home, fed up with his gloominess and New York Dolls obsession? Whatever it is, he repeats that "It's not my home, it's their home" and he's not welcome.

178

So whom is Morrissey riding with? This is left to the listener's imagination, so if you want to project yourself into this song, be prepared to die. He's sitting in the backseat of your car when you hear him say, "If a double-decker bus crashes into us," he's looking forward to dying by your side, which would be a heavenly way to die (says you). No, wait, it should be a ten-ton truck that slams into your car. It'll kill you both and the "pleasure, the privilege is mine."

If you're a woman who's driving Morrissey around, you should be proud. The women in his lyrics are normally intangible sirens bent on luring him to his death on the rocky shores of dirty lust. He usually storms away pouting or else tells them that he's "not like that." But here, Morrissey must really like you, because he's willing to let you die with him.

The next stanza has Morrissey asking you to take him anywhere. He doesn't care where. Why, the two of you could go to a Cure concert and heckle Robert Smith. He mentions having been in a "darkened underpass" earlier contemplating suicide, but says he couldn't ask for assistance. This was right about the time you decided to enter this Smiths song and offer him a ride. "Take me home, take me anywhere," he pleads. He never wants to go home because it's so much better "driving in your car."

The chorus returns again, as Morrissey repeats his wish for a double-decker bus *and* a ten-ton truck to smash into your car (the guy certainly knows the meaning of "follow through"). The song finishes up with Morrissey singing the title repeatedly until the fade. By this time, you can pull over and order him out of your car, or if you're a true Smiths fan, keep driving until a bus plows into you.

WHY IT'S CREEPY

I know what you're thinking. This is a love song? Yes, it is, albeit one from Morrissey, the best you'll ever get from him. Sure, it's a great tune, the music is sparkly and infectious, the vocals are nice, the rhythm section is solid, and the synth strings are a neat touch. But Morrissey's never been much of a romanticist and his sexuality is more debatable than who wrote the Dead Sea Scrolls.

From everything written about Morrissey, he'll probably never settle down with another individual for the long term. That kind of commitment is too solid, too routine. He finds love and companionship in alienation, not Match.com. It's perfectly logical for him to ride around in a car with someone he just met while hoping they both get crushed under the wheels of a truck. The Smiths were noted for handing out flower bouquets to audiences at their shows; it's telling that Morrissey would offer a beautiful gift that's destined to die in a few days.

In the end, his passion comes from a fleeting glance, an ephemeral encounter, a car that's about to be flattened. For many of us, this is unerringly creepy, but to Morrissey it's the reason heaven knows he's miserable now. He couldn't be happier about it.

VERMILION & VERMILION PT. 2

Words and music by 0, 1, 2, 3, 4, 5, 6, 7, and 8
Performed by Slipknot
Released 2004
(No. 17 in U.S. modern rock chart, No. 31 in UK)

ATTENTION, METAL bands: stop inventing subgenres already. I'm freaking exhausted. I've already sampled speed metal, death metal, glam metal, thrash metal, industrial metal, and ambient metal. Now I find there's goth metal, funk metal, progressive metal, doom metal, black metal, avant-garde metal, power metal, symphonic metal, groove metal, Nu metal, and metalcore. (If anyone can tell the difference between death metal and doom metal, I'll buy you a cadaver.) There's even folk metal. Is Joan Baez biting off bat heads now? And what the hell is Viking metal? Why aren't Vikings out sacking and pillaging like they're supposed to? Don't tell me—they're too busy learning barre chords.

I'm calling a moratorium on this. No more metal genres, be it sludge metal, plague metal, ventriloquist metal, Fifth and Main metal, or three-bean salad metal. The only one I'll consider is beer metal. I like beer.

The preceding rant was inspired by the many hours I spent listening to metal bands while looking for creepy love songs. Amid the blackness I stumbled over Slipknot, a nine-piece band whose music is labeled Nu metal. I'm accepting this because I don't know what it means. Slipknot is unique in that the group features three drummers and a turntable operator along with the usual guitar/bass/drums blitzkrieg. Onstage the members wear dark coveralls and monstrous handmade masks so that they look like a highway work crew from *The Hills Have Eyes*.

Finally, everyone in Slipknot goes by a number, i.e., No. 8 on vocals, No. 4 on rhythm guitar, No. 1 on drums, and No. 12 on virgin sacrificing.

Within Slipknot's metallic catalog is the two-part song "Vermilion," a dark ode to a spooky girl who lives her entire life in time-lapse. I say this because both parts come with their own phantasmagoric music videos starring an actress who moves around like one of those ghosts in *The Ring* and *The Grudge*, all stop-motion spasmodic. What's freakier is how much she resembles a hungover undead Olsen twin. In other words, she looks like an Olsen twin.

THE SONG

As there are two parts to "Vermilion," each part its own song, I'm going through them without the usual line-by-line fussiness. Part one is a full-blown grenade assault; part two is a disturbing acoustic affair a la Folk Night at the Thorazine Coffee House. Part one pummels, part two drains. Part one is creepy, part two is ultracreepy. Neither song makes a lot of sense lyrically. For clarity's sake, both should be listened to in a darkened room while visualizing Mary-Kate Olsen wearing a burial shroud as she runs screaming from a sandwich. (You can visualize Ashley instead, if you want. Like it matters.)

Part one blasts open with oil derrick guitars while lead singer No. 8 coolly talk-sings of a girl dressed in "all the rings," a fragile and devious creature with nervous hands that press against her temples. The night arrived when "she came home FOREVER" (caps mine; you'll understand when you hear it). Part two, which slightly resembles Pink Floyd's "Goodbye Blue Skies," offers autumn-tinged acoustic guitar and spare piano that leads us from one bare tree to another. Here, No. 8 is resigned as he laments a girl whose torment and pain cover him. He wants her to himself but doesn't know what to do. She "makes me sad," No. 8 claims in both parts.

If you're confused about what in the hell is going on, you should be. Both parts of "Vermilion" follow in the long tradition of songs whose lyrics we don't quite understand but we can pretend we do (I blame Bob Dylan). You can still visualize Mary-Kate's gaunt visage, bloodless skin tone, spasmodic gestures, and (fingers crossed) eventual casting in yet another remake of a Japanese horror film.

Part one continues its jackhammering while part two glides like wind on David Lynch's meadow. Part one finds her a "solemn hypnotic" (as opposed to those giddy hypnotic types), a "Dahlia" who makes him nervous and "perverse." Seeing her only freaks him out more. Part two is more plaintive, where the Olsen apparition is everything, a song that "no one sings" (until now). She's taken on mythic proportions, becoming something he has to believe in. No. 8 is still sad, too. Not even a *Full House* marathon will cheer him up.

Part one adds a twisted bridge where No. 8 recalls what drew him to her in the first place. He describes it as an "aphid attraction." Must be one of the Nu metal things. Uh-oh, she's carving his name on his face now. It's a "pheromone cult." Part two has no bridge, no face carving, no aphids, no pheromone cult. Cool. Let's move on.

Where the two parts join together is in the mantralike chorus that appears in both songs. Vocalist No. 8, with the help of percussionists No. 3 and No. 6, sings how he "won't let this build up inside of me." It seems to be a big priority since it's repeated a lot. I'm guessing it's insanity because in part one, it follows with screaming references to slaves and masters, of which No. 8 claims he's both. He exists via a need to "self-oblige," a behavioral trait I'm dying to try out to see what it's like. Meanwhile, she's become something inside him that he despises. Part two simply finds him choking while being torn into pieces.

The buildup denial repeats again (and again) in both until a surprise coda reveals that "she isn't real" and he can't make her real. It too is repeated, possibly to ward off her ghost, until both songs end in their respective fashion, part one in a crash of overheated crunch, part two with the slow fade of a final chord.

WHY IT'S CREEPY

Because both songs are lyrically solipsistic, it's difficult to pinpoint why they're so creepy to listen to. It's more of an overall feeling you get from either song, be it the snarl of "Vermilion" or the resignation of "Vermilion pt. 2." I find the latter song particularly unsettling because it casts a blanket of dread over the listener with its sluggish tempo, woody acoustic guitars, and desperation. To get my drift, watch the music videos for both "Vermilion" and "Vermilion pt. 2." Both feature the Olsen doppelganger in emotional torment, in the big city (L.A., of course) in "Vermilion," seemingly dead while floating eerily in a windy meadow in "Vermilion pt. 2." Both are visually nightmarish.

As creepy goes, Slipknot is somewhat of a no-brainer, since its music rarely strays outside the death and disintegration paradigm of metal songs. Still, I hacked through Slipknot's morass of distortion, bile, and janitorial Halloween biz to find proficient musicians (their drummers are amazing), songs with actual melodies, and a lead vocalist who doesn't constantly shriek as though he's got an adder crawling up his colon. Granted, I don't want these guys showing up at my house to do yard work anytime soon, but I'll give them their due. As for other metal groups, while I found some intriguing (see Rammstein's "Marry Me"), most of them bored me with their down-tuned axes and riff-redundant songs that make you think your CD player is skipping. At least Slipknot creeped me out for real.

MARRY ME (HEIRATE MICH)

Words and music by Till Lindemann, Richard Kruspe, Paul
Landers, Flake Lorenz, Oliver Riedel, and Christoph Schneider
Performed by Rammstein
Released 1995 (no chart position)

ACHTUNG!! ICH mag flaumige Häschenkaninchen!!!

Is it me or does everything sound intimidating in German? I
just said that I like fluffy bunny rabbits. How many of you
thought I was planning to invade Belgium?

I ponder this because I'm watching a streaming video of Till
Lindemann, the charismatic vocalist of the theatrical German
band Rammstein as he stalks a Berlin concert stage bellowing
"*Heirate Mich!*" The rest of the band echo with "*Hei! Hei! Hei!*"
The teeming crowd chants along while the music pounds like a
collapsing factory. It's very menacing and Visigoth-like. Viewer
comments posted under the video window nervously ask the
same thing: what is he saying?

Heirate Mich. Marry Me.

While you're reveling in the irony, note that there's a slight
catch. The girl receiving Lindemann's proposal is a decomposing
corpse he's just dug up out of the ground. He's come to "*was
noch übrig ist,*" take what's left of you. *Ich bin ein Necrophile.*

I admit that Rammstein is new to me even though the band has
been around since 1993. Here in the U.S., the only German music
you'll ever hear is either Mozart or the Scorpions. The latter don't
even sing in German. ("Rock You Like *ein grosser Wind*"?) When
I have dabbled in so-called kraut rock, it mostly sounded like
Tangerine Dream with a lot of Moog/Oberheim whacking and
programmed drums. Germany practically invented trance music,
starting back in the early seventies with works like "Autobahn,"

a twenty-minute electronica song by Kraftwerk that was released as a four-minute single. Translated, the lyrics are "We are driving on the Autobahn, we are driving on the Autobahn, we are driving on the Autobahn." I think it's about driving on the Autobahn.

But now my narrow world has been widened. Rammstein ("Ramming Stone") is an industrial metal band made up of six German musicians who made the radical choice of actually singing in German (most German rock groups try to sing in English). This didn't compromise their international appeal, and the band enjoys a substantial following, especially in Europe and Asia—in countries where nobody understands a thing they say. Their cornea-melting live shows include exploding microphones, custard-spewing dildos (don't ask) and enough flamethrowers to burn down the Alps. To say their music is dark is like saying the airline industry has a few flaws. Rammstein's songs explore grim industrial themes, i.e., death, war, tyranny, hearing someone sing about the Autobahn, etc., so it's no surprise to find a necrophilia song in their anthology; I would've been surprised not to. I'm not a fan of most industrial groups, because I find their nihilism boring (yeah, yeah, life is futile, I get it), and I was expecting the same reaction listening to Rammstein's grotesque "Heirate Mich." Instead I came away strangely compelled and a budding fan.

THE SONG

Over an eerie drone, vocalist Lindemann begins by singing in third person as a way to set up the song's premise. "You see him sneaking," he growls, describing a mysterious figure that haunts a church cemetery at night. We learn it is a man, alone and in mourning for over a year, sleeping "every night near her stone." Lindemann's voice, by the way, can only be described as subterranean. He makes Brad Roberts from Crash Test Dummies sound like a castrati.

The drone ends and the band crash into a pummeling beat that continues for a full minute. In the video, Lindemann stays kneeling on the stage, staring expressionlessly as he changes personalities. When he resumes singing, it's in the first person as he adopts the persona of the grieving grave sleeper. He notes how the "bells are asleep" and that "a red cock" sits on a fence (it's a rooster; grow up already). These are familiar sights to him as he clearly does this every night.

While the band pounds away, Lindemann begins digging, digging, yet another part of his nightly ritual. He is unearthing his love's coffin so he can see what remains *"von dem Gesicht das mir gelacht,"* of that face that once smiled at me. The minor tonic chord crashing suddenly shifts to the dominant while Lindemann roars of his loneliness, "an animal among beasts," because her death let her escape him a second time. You can actually hear the chorus approaching and can't wait to hear what it is.

"HEIRATE MICH!" The crowd of thirty thousand strong chants along, bobbing like Saxon pogo sticks. It's loud, frenzied, and in German, so if you stumbled into the middle of it without previous knowledge, you'd think, *oh great, here we go again.* But no, it's a marriage proposal to an emaciated corpse and it sends chills down your vertebrae.

The band drops the volume to subtemblor level as Lindemann pries open the coffin. As the moon glows above him, he *"deinen kalten Mund geküßt,"* kisses her cold lips. Now the *eww* factor comes into play as he lifts the body out of the coffin. Her skin tears like paper while her limbs fall off her torso. The blast before the chorus returns as Lindemann the lonely animal works the crowd into the chant.

"HEIRATE MICH!!" (Hei! Hei! Hei! Hei!)

There's not much remaining of her, so Lindemann seduces what's left. The night is sweltering and *"wir sind nackt,"* we are naked. Suddenly, the dawn breaks and the rooster crows, forcing an end to his grisly reunion. A frustrated Lindemann decapitates the bird before fleeing. The chanting chorus returns one last time.

"*Heirate Mich!!*" The song ends suddenly with a last "*Hei!*" reverberating in the air.

WHY IT'S CREEPY

Wow, I said to myself, this is one of the most disgusting songs I've ever experienced. Why did I love it so much? Is it the obvious tenderness behind the necrophile's actions? The virtuosity of the musicians? Lindemann's subhuman basso profundo and the fact that he has more stage presence kneeling in silence than a dozen Chris Martins writhing in front of a piano? Why do I admire these Teutonic sickos and think they're one of most innovative music acts I've heard in years? I don't even like industrial music that much, all that tedious distortion and weekend anarchist ennui. Rammstein doesn't need my support. They can sell out a stadium in Sydney to a mass of Aussies who couldn't conjugate a German verb to save their vegemite. So then what was it?

It was the language.

Let me say, I don't speak German. My familiarity with German culture is limited to reading the subtitles of Fassbinder films featuring alienated Berliners who mumble existential gobbledygook. What a chuckle buffet those are. When I retrieved both the German and translated English lyrics to "Heirate Mich" off the Web, I lined them up side by side to keep track for fear I'd stumble out of the song and onto the Autobahn (one more time: "We're driving on the Autobahn, we're driving on the Autobahn"). So while I struggled to keep up, the guttural percussive quality of the German lyrics fascinated me. It completely fits Rammstein's music, almost like another instrument, especially when it comes pouring out of Lindemann's throat (what a scary figure that guy is).

As for reading the English translation, something unique occurs. Normally when you translate song lyrics, the phrases feel awkward and nothing rhymes any more. On the other hand, "Heirate Mich" in English becomes a haunting free verse tale of loneliness, obsession, and the darkest, creepiest form of eternal love. As much as I tried to resist the song, "Heirate Mich" blew me away. I loved it.

The Germans have always been geniuses at being twisted. It varies in quality, of course. For every Bertolt Brecht and "Threepenny Opera," there was a *fanatiker* screaming at rallies while ordering his minions to invade countries without an invitation. Again, I think it's their aggressive language. If the Germans had switched to speaking French back in the 1930s, they would've just insulted the rest of Europe, not blitzkrieged it.

A coda: "Heirate Mich" first appeared on Rammstein's 1995 CD *Herzeleid* and it was the only song in which they did not print the lyrics in German. They decided to include them in a different language because, they figured, it would look less offensive.

The words are printed in French.

CODE BLUE

Words and music by Jack Grisham and Ron Emory
Performed by T.S.O.L.
Released 1981 (no chart position)

BEFORE RESEARCHING this book I'd never thought much about necrophilia beyond wondering who was sleeping with Kate Moss. I did discover that while humans largely abhor it, necrophilia occurs often in nature. One naturalist observed a mallard duck copulate with a deceased duck for seventy-five minutes. I found this interesting if only because I had no idea naturalists have that much free time on their hands.

Musicwise, songs about necrophilia have a limited legacy. Alice Cooper offered up two catchy numbers during the seventies with "Cold Ethyl" and "I Love the Dead," both intentionally tongue-in-cheek. It wasn't until later that the, um, Golden Age of Corpse Anthems began with so-called "death metal" groups like Cannibal Corpse, Necromancer, Entombed, Obituary, blah blah. Death metal necrophilia songs tend to feature graves, shrouds, and rotting corpses (OK, *every* death metal song features them), yet it's difficult not to roll your eyes at it. I love Halloween, but when you observe it every day, it's time to get a hobby.

I considered abandoning the whole *Romancing the Bones* theme until I stumbled across "Code Blue," a pounding necrophilia song by the L.A. punk band T.S.O.L. (True Sounds of Liberty). What makes "Code Blue" stand out from the rest of the cadaver catalogue is how narrowly it walks the line between grotesque and hilarious. T.S.O.L. were part of California's Orange County punk music scene during the eighties, and developed a small but rabid cult following. The band is largely defunct nowadays, but its reputation lies partly in "Code Blue," because the song became a minor underground hit (in the punk world, this means an inordinately large number of people liked it without ever buying it).

THE SONG

Analyzing songs about people boning corpses is something I'm new at. If there's an editorial paradigm to follow, I'm unaware of it. All I can say is this song educated me a lot about the dynamic of boy-meets-corpse relationships. "Code Blue" opens with eight bars of medium-tempo skater rock before the band violently switches to a frenetic punk beat while vocalist Jack Grisham sets up an unusual adolescent issue.

> *I never got along with the girls at my school,*
> *Filling me up with all their morals and their rules*
> *They'd pile all their problems on my head*
> *I'd rather go out and fuck the dead*

First off, this doesn't sound like much of a love song; but I found that with necrophilia anthems, you can't be picky. Instead we have an adolescent protagonist who's annoyed with his female classmates, finding them to be judgmental and pious. He's more comfortable locating corpses of dead girls with whom he can perform intercourse. I'm guessing there's a motivation behind this:

> *'Cause I can do what I want and they won't complain*
> *I wanna fuck, I wanna fuck the dead*

Hmm, OK. Our protagonist has commitment issues. Necrophiliacs are usually afraid of social interaction and prefer the calmness that comes with being around dead people. I for one want to know where he meets them.

The music unexpectedly returns to the medium-tempo intro during which we hear:

Middle of the night so silently
I creep on over to the mortuary
Lift up the casket and fiddle with the dead
Their cold blue flesh makes me turn red

Now I didn't know any of this but it certainly makes sense. The trick to meeting dead chicks is finding a mortuary with a twenty-four-hour open-door policy ("Touch what we got, before they rot"). This would be a useful guide for other budding corpse aficionados who don't want the sweat and hassle of grave robbing.

At this point an actual bridge, that rarest of things in a punk song, appears, whereupon the lyrics to the chorus are expanded:

Cause I can do what I want and they won't complain
I wanna fuck I wanna fuck the dead
And I don't even care how she died . . .
But I like it better if she smells of formaldehyde!

I'm wondering how accurate this is. Granted, formaldehyde keeps a corpse preserved, but wouldn't the smell compromise the mood somewhat? If you were a die-hard necrophiliac, wouldn't you prefer the festering odor of a decaying body? Just a thought . . .

The song switches tempo again, returning to its pogo pounding while Grisham qualifies his reasoning:

Never on the rag or say, leave me alone
They don't scream and they don't moan
Won't even cry if I shoot in their hair
Lying on the table she smiles and she stares

Although I'm fairly certain corpses don't have monthly cycles, I'm not sure they're able to crack a smile. But perhaps our protagonist is so gifted at wooing dead females, they can't help falling for his charms.

After a repeat of the chorus, something about fucking the dead, the song blasts to a finish, clocking in at a brisk 2:09, a very efficient use of time when you consider how much you learn in the song's duration.

WHY IT'S CREEPY

Why is this song creepy? Well, despite the obvious shock value, one can hear an amazing amount of dynamics for such a short song. The tempo changes and unexpected chord structures give the song a raw sophistication while never compromising its anarchic energy. "Code Blue" could easily be turned into a power pop song providing the tempo stayed consistent and the lyrics weren't about, well, fucking a corpse. The other surprising thing is how easily you can understand the lyrics, not a common attribute of punk/grindcore/death metal songs. T.S.O.L. experimented with different music genres far more than their contemporaries like the Germs and Black Flag, utilizing art rock, blues, thrash, and other styles. It didn't always work and it tested the loyalty of their fans, but one must credit them for trying.

Whether T.S.O.L. ever recorded another necrophilia song, I hope not, because it'd be like painting your parachute a different color before skydiving out of the plane. Necrophilia is a very narrow gimmick, so there's not much room for variation (if any of you can find room, please keep it to yourself). All I know is that I'll never look at ducks the same way again.

I AM STRETCHED ON YOUR GRAVE

Based on traditional Irish poem "Táim sinte ar do thuama,"
English translation by Frank O'Connor, music by Phillip King
Arranged by Sinéad O'Connor
Performed by Sinéad O'Connor
Released 1990 (no chart position)

DESPITE MY surname, I'm not Irish, but I love their slang and I intend to use it freely over the next few pages. I especially admire Irish melancholy. Nobody mopes better than the Irish, which explains why you never see Bono doing stand-up. But while "Danny Boy" is the sing-along lament at the pub, I gamely put my nicker on our last corpse-love song, "I Am Stretched on Your Grave," one of the creepiest songs to ever find a brogue. Based on the old poem "Táim sinte ar do thuama," this haunting work has been crooned by many an Irish singer over the years, but the best version comes from that qweer bit o' skirt named Sinéad O'Connor.

If you remember, Sinéad was once the Next Big Thing back in 1990. Her second album *I Do Not Want What I Haven't Got* went to No. 1 with the help of her cover of "Nothing Compares 2 U," written by Prince, the world's only purple leprechaun. But bless her, our bonnie Sinéad went off her nut and ripped up a photo of Pope John Paul II on that unfunny shite of a comedy show *Saturday Night Live*. After she got jeered off stage at a Bob Dylan tribute concert as though she were a Bombay shitehawk, Sinéad's career went into the bogs for a while and has yet to fully recover.

'Tis unfair. Sure, she seems to go off her head at times and who knows what's up with that bald skull of hers, but she's a feckin' fine musician with one of the most distinctive voices in pop music. "Nothing Compares 2 U" is a wee bit overrated, but listen to her whole catalog and it's clear that Ms. O'Connor was (and still is) a true talent. As far as crazy goes, well, she's not half a mentaller as Björk.

THE SONG

The original poem tells of a grief-stricken young man whose true love has died, so he goes to her grave every night, sprawls across it, and yearns to touch her again (today he'd just date her sister). While "I Am Stretched on Your Grave" has been performed in various ways, from sublime a cappella (Kate Rusby) to full-blown electronica bombast (Dead Can Dance), Sinéad's version is almost oxymoronic, combining a drum sample from James Brown's "Funky Drummer" and subtle synth bass with a coda of Irish fiddles. The resulting mixture can only be described as Gaelic funk.

It opens with a lone drum kit laying down a hypnotic groove for eight bars until Sinéad's ethereal voice sings how she's stretched out over the grave of a dead lover, yearning to shove her hand through the soil and grasp the corpse's hand. A simple two-note bass line appears, making syncopated stabs every other bar as the drums clip along. She mournfully wishes for them to be together again while noting that "I smell of the earth and am worn by the weather." She's torn up with grief for "a girl I loved as a child." This stanza suggests Sinéad's a bean flicker, but as she's changed sexual orientation more often than Van Halen has lead singers, it's more likely she just sang the words as translated. At this point a wave of instruments would normally come crashing in, but Sinéad, bless her, wisely keeps the drum-and-bass bed going beneath her while she recalls a past time when her girl was still alive and the two of them got lost in the woods one night. Fortunately they "did what was right" and made sure the deceased girl's "maidenhead" remained pure. This implies that Sinéad, being no manky spunkskip, chose not to take the girl's virginity—i.e., go up the rasher while pawing her funbags—as they lay huddled together in the cold woods. The girl instead dies later with her purity intact, leaving Sinéad with no choice but to go to the grave, undress, and perhaps flah her gee-box with a flagon. Aye, but her midnight vigil is interrupted by the arrival of various priests and friars who approach her "with dread" as she lies atop the grave.

This is my favorite part of the storyline, because I'd mortgage my house for the opportunity to witness a half-dozen clerics come across Sinéad O'Connor as she drops a hand on her womble. Scandalized, the party of monks escorts her out of the cemetery, lecturing her on the sins of diddlin' the flange. Aye, but the next night, Sinéad returns yet again: "I am stretched on your grave and will lie there forever . . ." The song ends with a set of Irish fiddles playing a churning reel over the funky bass/drum track before coming to sudden stop.

WHY IT'S CREEPY

Seriously, Sinéad's rendition of "I Am Stretched on Your Grave" is near brilliant, with its ghostly vocals and mesmerizing minimalist production. It completely ignores the standard verse/chorus/bridge structure of songwriting and instead concentrates on the poem's narrative while creating a dark aura around the listener. Ordinarily this results in a plodding drone of melodic wash, but here it works wonderfully. "I Am Stretched on Your Grave" is easily one of the strongest tracks on her second album, which contains several excellent songs including the rocking "Emperor's New Clothes." While not technically a necrophilia song since we're dealing with a chaste corpse, it is nonetheless creepy and unforgettable, by turns both beautiful and disturbing. For the best results, take a few shots of Jameson, turn off the lights, put on the headphones, and let the whole song drape over you like a ghost's shroud. If you're really brave, try to imagine a nude Irish vocalist with a shaved head lying on a freshly dug grave as she thrums her minge under a full moon. Now there's a bag o' shwag.

THOSE FREAKING BUTTERFLY SONGS

FOUR BUTTERFLY SONGS

BUTTERFLY

Words and music by Mariah Carey and Walter Afanasieff
Performed by Mariah Carey
Released 1997 (No. 22 in UK)

BUTTERFLY KISSES

Words and music by Bob Carlisle and Randy Thomas
Performed by Bob Carlisle
Released 1997 (No. 17 in U.S.)

BUTTERFLY

Words and music by Kevin Martin, Peter Klett,
Bardi Martin, and Scott Mercado
Performed by Candlebox
Released 1995 (no chart position)

BUTTERFLY

Words and music by Rivers Cuomo
Performed by Weezer
Released 1996 (no chart position)

ACCORDING TO entomologists, there are an estimated seventeen to eighteen thousand species of butterfly around the world. Every one of them is presently working in a pop song.

When a butterfly isn't being tossed around one of Lenny Kravitz's seventies Xeroxed love ballads, it's lulling kids to sleep in a Lisa Loeb children's song. One is them is noodling a where-am-I sax solo on a Herbie Hancock jazz fusion piece, while another is fluttering to a Jamiroquai dance funk number. Wait, take the kids back to the house; Michael Jackson just entered the room with a butterfly track off his *Invincible* CD. It's his family's favorite album since they're the only ones who bought it. Plus there's Screaming Trees, Andy Williams, Darius Rucker, Yanni, Sarah Vaughan, Sonic Youth, Pete Droge, Wes Montgomery, Tiffany, Amps for Christ, Nozmo King, Ass Ponys, ad infinitum. Artists who have nothing in common with each other are kindred spirits because they did songs about butterflies.

What's with this *Lepidoptera* obsession? Why are locusts, bees, and mantises getting the short shrift while butterflies are juggling offers from Sonic Youth and Tiffany? Perhaps their staggering number of species lets butterflies come pre-customized to the needs of any artist. A polydamas swallowtail form-flits effortlessly into a Tori Amos track, while a martial scrub-hairstreak drops the hammer with the Cult. Massive Attack and a pacific checkerspot work nicely together on an electronica beat. Kylie Minogue shimmies with a Danube clouded sulpher. The Verve can't do without their stinky leaf wing.

Butterflies are quiet, too. While an errant fly will drive you nuts buzzing against the inside of a window, butterflies make nary a sound as they bob about aimlessly. They don't bite, sting, or roll dung into little balls. They don't eat your house, build hives in your garage, or hang under your dog's chin for a month sucking blood until they're the size of a grape. They don't spread Lyme disease. They don't devour crops. Butterflies are pretty, colorful, and mute. What could be better?

The one thing consistent about butterfly songs is that they're nearly all metaphorical. Nobody sings literally about a butterfly's life. How tough could it be? Flutter, drink nectar, flutter, flutter, eat nectar, flutter. Unless it ends up pinned to a wall or devoured by a chameleon, a butterfly has it pretty easy. But when we give one human attributes, everything changes. Now the butterfly can get drunk after work, cheat on his taxes, and screw around behind his wife's back (I've yet to hear a butterfly song that addresses any of these, but whatever; I can dream). The typical butterfly song is about someone being set free, and not in a parolee sense. The singer is trying to be altruistic by allowing the other person a chance to test her wings and fly off to explore life. If she comes back, it's because she failed miserably at it.

But while there's an inherent touchy-feely aspect to most butterfly songs, ironically you'll find just as many rock, metal, and alternative bands doing them as you will Jewel. These are the *Silence of the Lambs* butterfly songs, where the butterfly is captured, cornered, or being stalked. Some outfits relish burying an Aphrodite fritillary under a tidal wave of fuzz and wailing. The butterfly becomes a hapless victim or even a coconspirator in the band's quest for world domination.

There are at present around seventeen hundred different songs available for download entitled "Butterfly" or some variation thereof. Promotional literature from my publisher claims I listened to all seventeen hundred titles before making my selection of the four creepiest. Well, if you think I'm *that* insane . . . No, instrumentals were immediately disqualified, as were spoken word, old jazz standards, and anything seemingly conceived by a lunatic, e.g., "The Early Sunrise Death of the Turquoise Swamp Butterflies, Opus 11, No. 33" from the album *Requiem for the Death of the Last Butterflies, Opus 11*. I scanned the remaining titles and looked for the obvious novelty numbers like "Butterfly Labes," "Diapertime Butterfly," etc. Gone. I was left with nearly a thousand. Who has an idiotic name? HeavyMetalDad, Quit Your Dayjob, undadog, you're outta here. Still I barely made a dent. I gave in and began listening.

THE SONGS

The four butterfly songs I selected come courtesy of pop diva Mariah Carey, country artist Bob Carlisle, metal outfit Candlebox, and alt-rock heroes Weezer. I felt it was important to feature butterfly songs from various genres so we could see how each artist creates them. Plus, I wanted to shove Mariah Carey and Candlebox into the same room together and see what happened.

Mariah Carey, "Butterfly"

Mariah Carey's "Butterfly" is the title cut off her 1997 album of the same name, and it hews the closest to the traditional butterfly song—i.e., setting someone "free" so he can test his wings, fly through life, die on the grill of a speeding truck, etc. It contains all the trappings of a Mariah ballad, including the overproduced R&B arrangements and faux-gospel choir that shows up at the chorus like sharks around a sinking ocean liner. Mariah sings how her butterfly can't be kept "under glass" and that it's time to open her hands and "watch you rise." The chorus strains under the weight of twenty-five redundant altos as they all sing about how we should spread our wings and prepare to fly because "you have become a butterfly." This, of course, is yet another use of the stupid phrase "spread your wings and fly." If I'm genetically equipped to be sporting wings, I don't need to be reminded to spread them first.

Mariah, of course, hopes the butterfly will come back. If it returns then they were meant to be. If not, well, fuck you, butterfly. As the slick music oozes along, she throws in references to wild horses unbridled and flying towards the sun "abandonedly," the first time I've seen "abandoned" dressed up in adverb clothing. The song's chorus repeats again so we get to hear the "spread your wings" directive *nine* times, lest we miss it. It's a long ballad, nearly five minutes in length, but at least we get those flying instructions drilled into our heads.

Bob Carlisle, "Butterfly Kisses"

This MOR barrel of corn syrup is more like a death's-head moth dressed in treacle. It won the 1997 Grammy for Best Country Song, proof once again that the members of the Grammy committee vote while taking in the view of their own sphincters. The song is a sappy ballad about a father who relishes the "butterfly kisses" that his daughter gives him as she's growing up. For those unaware, a butterfly kiss is when you press your eye against another person's cheek and blink your eyelashes on their skin. It's the optometrist's version of a high five. As this requires eyelashes as long as a Portuguese man-of-war, I've never attempted it with anyone. I'm funny that way.

"Butterfly Kisses" begins with the sound of children playing while a tediously sloooowwww intro dawdles its way for eight bars. Carlisle sings of watching his little girl praying by her bed as she gets ready for night-night. The butterfly in this song has been reduced to a stunt, a gimmick, a strange ritual performed by people who have Venus flytraps where their eyelids should be. Carlisle happily gives her butterfly kisses while he sticks little white flowers in her hair. They do sweet father-daughter things together like pony rides until she's suddenly sixteen and looking more like "her momma" every day. He's still giving her butterfly kisses and sticking white flowers in her hair. She's looking forward to moving out one day. So am I.

By the end of the song, the little girl's all grown up and about to marry. The butterfly is waiting to get his dignity back. Before she walks down the aisle, the girl agrees to give Daddy her first butterfly kiss and they shove their faces forward like dueling elks. Swish, swish. The song mercifully ends, leaving your life six minutes shorter.

Candlebox, "Butterfly"

Those guys in Candlebox bring their own mutant solipsistic "Butterfly" to the table, beginning with muted electric guitar picking as vocalist Kevin Martin quietly lays out truncated phrases—"Lies to, love to, feel it all"—while working up his Seattle ennui. The butterfly in this song is (wait for it) a form of escape, something that will take a confused grunge band and get them away from the snobby purists who think they're sellouts. There's not a lot of love in this song, but what do you expect? They're from Seattle.

"Fly us home, butterfly," goes the heavy chorus, while Martin asks for a simple change. The song's lyrics never go beyond interrupted phrases—"Set it for, to kill for, kill for you,"—and the tension builds like the caffeine content in their nuclear coffee. He's willing to kill for his butterfly, sending our winged friend into a major power trip. *No one's ever offered to kill for me*, it thinks, *but since you brought it up, go take care of that "Butterfly Kisses" guy*. The music slams into its fullest grunge pile-on as the band members wail for the butterfly to fly them home. Then more dashed phrases appear—"Every life is taken, what for? I've dropped to . . ."—A complete sentence is harder to find in this song than a major chord. The butterfly loads them on his narrow thorax and flies them home, leaving the Marshall stacks behind. The song ends with the defeated chanting as the guitars build to a wall of fuzz before violently coming to a stop. The butterfly dons his flannel and heads for Happy Hour.

Weezer, Butterfly

Our last creepy "Butterfly" song comes from Weezer and their 1996 release *Pinkerton*, a concept album supposedly based on the Puccini opera *Madame Butterfly*. In the opera an American naval officer named Pinkerton takes a Japanese girl nicknamed Butterfly as his young bride. He later abandons her and marries an American woman. Butterfly kills herself (I just saved you four hours). Weezer vocalist and songwriter, the goofy celibate Rivers Cuomo, used the opera as a template for the songs on *Pinkerton*, closing it with the acoustic "Butterfly."

The music is stark, simple acoustic guitar, which Cuomo strums while he recalls going outside with his "momma's mason jar" to catch a "lovely butterfly." The next morning he looks in the jar to find his pet butterfly "withered all away." He's filled with regret and says he's sorry for what he did. Here, the butterfly is a suicide, being a representation of the Asian child bride who kills herself after being abandoned. The butterfly in the jar was captured and put on display but later ignored. Of course, the thousands of Weezer fans who bought *Pinkerton* probably never got the connection to the opera and figured Cuomo was just being Cat Stevens.

The lyrics take a harsh turn as Cuomo sings how he can "smell you on my hand" and that he can't wash the scent off. "If I'm a dog, then you're a bitch," he intones, while filling out his application for Harvard. Maybe he needs some fantasies, he thinks, "a life of chasing butterflies." Apparently, killing just one isn't enough. No wonder he took a vow of celibacy. Still, he's filled with regret, saying he did what his body told him to. Now the butterfly is a ghost who slips away.

The song ends as quietly as it began, with Cuomo repeating "I'm sorry, I'm sorry . . ."

WHY THEY'RE CREEPY

It's interesting that our four butterfly songs were all released within a year of each other. Apparently, the mid-nineties was a banner time for buggy butterfly songs, and I didn't even notice it until later. All four artists use the butterfly in their own creepy way. Mariah Carey's "Butterfly" is the most standard and overdone. The creepiness is in the bawling way she releases her butterfly, wailing five octaves while the choir goes all tabernacle soul on everything. It's something Mariah does a lot, and it gets tiresome. That she chose to do a butterfly song and then resorted to the most cliche imagery you could ever use was bad enough. Now she's standing in the field tossing the thing like it's a hand grenade while tearfully directing it to spread its wings and fly. It does, and it ain't comin' back anytime soon, either. It's not as though she's going to be alone, though; she still has the choir.

Carlisle's "Butterfly Kisses" is beyond redemption. By taking a cutesy gesture and writing a near-six-minute saccharine ballad about it, he reduces the butterfly to a quickie stunt. This song earns its bad-creep stripes by the unabashed sickly way he goes all gaga about flitting his eyelashes at her like a ravenous squid. I know, I know, it's a loving tribute from a father to his daughter, but the song's mawkish lyrics and overwrought delivery destroy any sublime charm it could've had. "Butterfly Kisses" is supposedly played at wedding receptions for fathers to dance to with their bride daughters. I cannot imagine who would request such a thing, except that they probably had "Every Breath You Take" played during the ceremony.

Candlebox's "Butterfly" gets its creepiness from its detached vocals, sludge guitar work, and half-finished lyrics that imply somebody's losing his grip. The butterfly takes on a rare savior-like role, as they continually ask it to fly them home. As stated earlier, there is no implied love theme in this song except for some leftover bitterness that's revealed at the end. It's the odd interruptions of thought that lend an unsettling air to the song and make you wonder how these guys ever order a pizza. The butterfly is the only normal one in the song.

As for Weezer, the more you know your Puccini, the creepier its "Butterfly" may sound. But even if you set that aside, the song is still a strange and unsettling work, with its references to withered bodies and ghosts that slip away. You can glean from Cuomo's apologies that something bad happened that went beyond a dead butterfly in a jar. His lashing out combined with his sorrowful regret tells the listener that he's forced the death of something beautiful to him that he was too self-absorbed to notice. Of the four acts, Weezer is by far the quirkiest, so we can expect they'd do something loopy like base an album on a 110-

year-old opera. But Cuomo sings so brokenly about his lost butterfly that it may be better to ignore the Puccini link and let the song creep you out on its own merits.

LITTLE DITTIES ABOUT ORAL SEX AND MASTURBATION

MY BOY LOLLIPOP

Words and music by Morris Levy, Robert Spencer,
and J. Roberts
Performed by Millie
Released 1964 (No. 2 in U.S., No. 2 in UK)

YOU KNOW the old "pat your head while rubbing your stomach" challenge? That's nothing. Try playing in a ska band.

The precursor to reggae, ska is typically described as a conscious mixture of American R&B and Caribbean calypso/mento music, developed in Jamaica in the 1950s. How polite; how academic. Now cut the crap and say what ska really is: a confused drummer mixed with a dozen rolled spliffs. Jamaican musicians invented it while trying to cover R&B tunes and simply played them wrong. The result was a nervous dance rhythm that resembled soul music with the hiccups.

To understand how tricky ska is to play, give this a try: count out four beats like this: 1-AND-2-AND-3-AND-4-AND-1, etc. in a fast tempo. As you count, tap your hand on the AND part of the beat (the upbeat), not on the numbers (downbeat). Now stop counting and sing your favorite song while trying to keep your hand tapping on the up beat. Odds are that you can't do it, proving that you're human. If you can do it, you're a genetic oddity.

The introduction of Jamaican ska music to the U.S. and Europe can be pinpointed to the release of Millie's cover of "My Boy Lollipop" in 1964. Originally an R&B song, "Lollipop" was a minor hit for Barbie Gaye in 1956, but it became a huge smash for the seventeen-year-old Millie (AKA Millie Small) under the tutelage of Chris Blackwell, the founder of Island Records. From an arrangement by legendary Jamaican guitarist Ernest Ranglin,

Millie's catchy version of "Lollipop" proved irresistible to Western ears unfamiliar with the choppy rhythms of ska. Today a pop classic, "My Boy Lollipop" is also extremely short and as lyrically profound as a traffic sign. Still, it deserves inclusion as one of our fifty-two creepy love songs for its coital ska beat and the alternative interpretation of the title and lyrics.

THE SONG

If you failed my ska test, you can try and tap along with "Lollipop" as long as you don't cheat and do it like a white man. As with most ska recordings, the upbeat is heavily accented on "Lollipop" via the pianist's right hand in unison with Raglin's popping guitar, a la boom-CHICK-boom-CHICK-boom-CHICK . . . After a bouncing intro, Millie sings (she practically chirps) how her boy lollipop makes her heart "go giddyup." While it's my nature to go medieval on anyone who'd rhyme "lollipop" with "giddyup," I shan't, because it was written in the fifties, when pop songs were more innocent and lollipops were a bigger part of the candy culture than they are today.

He's as sweet as candy, Millie sings about her lollipop beau, setting up the next glaring rhyme of him being her "sugar dandy." So not only is this guy an all-day sucker, he's also a dandy one to boot. Again, I'm not making fun, I'm just observing. By now you should've caught on just how obvious the lyrics are. If her next verse was "Never ever *leave me*" (which it is), complete the phrase "Because it would ____ ____." If you can't figure it out, I'll assume you're a proud graduate of the U.S. Public School System.

The song's B section consists of I love you's and I need you's, along with a reference to her wanting him "*to know*." Again, finish the phrase: "I'll never let ____ ____" (please tell me you can). After a harmonica solo that's so basic it makes Bob Dylan sound like Vladimir Horowitz, the opening chorus repeats, leading to the final line of him setting her "world *on fire*." OK, last rhyme challenge. If her heart's *on fire*, this

214

would make him her one ____. The song fades with the boom-CHICK-boom-CHICK rhythm still bounding inside your head like a dyslexic kangaroo.

WHY IT'S CREEPY

If the above analysis seems brief, it's because the song is slightly longer than a typical TV commercial and as deep as a sink. It could almost be considered a ditty except that for all its cutesiness, "My Boy Lollipop" is possibly one of the dirtiest songs to ever hit the charts. Of course, it takes a suspicious mind that sees double entendres everywhere to notice the perverted meaning to this song. Thankfully, I have that suspicious mind.

Allow me to present my case. First, I don't know any self-respecting guy who'd accept "lollipop" as a term of endearment from his girlfriend. ("Andy, Sarah, Nigel, this is my boyfriend Butch. But you can call him Lollipop. Everybody does.") If that's his real name, e.g. Lol E. Pop, then fine, we can assume he's probably someone who had to win a lot of playground fights. But it's more likely that "lollipop" is a euphemism, one as obvious as all the rhymes in the song. Oh yeah, she looovvves her boy's lollipop, it makes her giddyup, it's sweet like candy, it's sugar dandy. Need I go on?

Double entendres in song lyrics are not UFOs. They stand out like funnel clouds, and most genres of music, be they R&B, salsa, merengue, blues, rockabilly, etc., have employed double-meaning lyrics. "My Boy Lollipop" was originally an R&B song, a genre notorious for sexual innuendo, and when you add the humping rhythms of ska combined with the kittenish charm of Millie's voice, you have a deliciously suggestive creepy love song.

As for ska, most Jamaicans abandoned it for the slower beats of reggae and rocksteady after the cannabis kicked in, but it lived on in the seventies through UK groups like the Specials and the Beat. Today, there's always some earnest U.S. outfit trying to play ska. American critics love bands that play ska because they'll never achieve mainstream success. (Don't throw No Doubt at me, either. They didn't get big until they *stopped* playing ska.) The charm of ska's off-kilter rhythms is also its biggest Achilles' heel. It's a homogenous style of music that's difficult to vary in performance because once you do, it ain't ska any more. Regardless, ska made a trite R&B song into an infectious hit single, and when it's at full blast, ska is some of the happiest music to ever trip over a ground beat. Just remember, 1-AND-2-AND-3-AND-4-AND- . . .

I TOUCH MYSELF

Words and music by Christina Amphlett, Mark Entee,
Tom Kelly, and Billy Steinberg
Performed by Divinyls
Released 1991 (No. 4 in U.S., No. 10 in UK)

AS I write this, I'm watching a Divinyls music video. A seductive woman with thick hair the color of Russia glides around a set filled with bedroom props. She's singing an infectious post–New Wave rock track with so many hooks you could snare a school of fish with it. There might be a guy playing guitar with her; I'm not sure. Who cares? She keeps returning to that same line: "I touch myself . . ."

This is yet another reason to love and fear the Internet, when anybody can pull up an old music video of a nineties song about masturbation. Indeed, that's what Divinyls' 1991 hit "I Touch Myself" was about, and not in that sneaky Cyndi Lauper She Bop way, either. Even protozoa knew exactly what Divinyls were singing about, yet the song was so catchy that Baptist missionaries probably caught themselves humming along with it.

Divinyls were primarily the duo of singer Christina "Chrissy" Amphlett and guitarist Mark Entee, who hailed from Australia. Labeled a one-hit wonder in America, the group maintained a long career down under, releasing six albums and charting numerous Oz hits. Their sole crossover hit was "I Touch Myself."

That said, I now have to write about "I Touch Myself" without knowing any slang phrases for female masturbation beyond the Irish ones I used earlier. Sure, I know the male ones—choking the chicken, milking the snake, slapping the bishop, etc.—but I'll be damned if I can recall any for women, and I'm not Googling for them either. I don't even like the word masturbation. What drooling zoologist conceived that noun? Did mastodons practice it first, lying on their furry backs while singing "I Tusk Myself?" Therefore I'm going to make one up. Ready?

Pressing the buzzer.

THE SONG

Back to the video, which I'm still watching. It begins with a thumping, tension-laden guitar with the attention-deficit editing techniques of an MTV video before locking into a mid-tempo rock beat. The divine Chrissy with her hooded eyes and pursing lips wastes no time singing about what she's up to. "I love myself," she coos, while adding that she wants me to love her. The interactive requests continue as she searches herself (wink wink). I'm supposed to "find" her, or at least perform a thorough search. She's the kind of adoring chick every guy wants and probably won't find unless his last name comes with a Swiss bank account.

I'm at the chorus. She's telling me she doesn't want anyone else. She's pressing her buzzer now while claiming she's thinking about me. "I touch myself," she sings. I'm seriously considering moving to Australia. Suddenly the song's bridge appears. It's about ninety seconds early but I don't care. Two other sultry women have shown up, too, wearing gold lamé short shorts. All have buzzers to press. I'm learning that I'm the one who makes her "come running." I make her shine, I make her laugh, and she makes me write checks with lots of zeros. I'm all hers.

The guitarist is wearing a red frilly outfit seemingly stolen from Air Supply's dressing room. I want him to get the hell out of my sight line. Chrissy is closing her eyes now while imagining I'm with her. She tells me she would die if I ever ignored her. She adores me so much that she'll "get down on my knees" and do anything for me. I tell her to make the guitarist change that stupid outfit.

We're going through the chorus again. She's pressing her buzzer so much it's like gynecological Morse code. She's still thinking about me, too, only me. There are black-and-white insert shots of Chrissy lounging under a sheet with her hands wandering south of her equator. Good Lord, now she's talking to me. "I want you," she says in an adorable Aussie accent. "I touch myself." I put everything I own in her name (boy, is she gonna be disappointed later on).

The video is finishing up now. Chrissie's touched herself approximately thirty-eight times over the past four minutes while one of the gold lamé girls changed into a black fetish outfit with a riding crop. The erotic impact is muted, though, since the guitarist is still dressed up like Air Supply. The track fades with Chrissie repeating over and over, "I touch myself, I honestly do."

WHY IT'S CREEPY

Ignore the above heading. While there are few if any hit songs as erotically charged as "I Touch Myself," I can honestly say it's not that creepy, even if others may disagree. If I was an honorable man, I would've excluded it from the book, but I'm not and I won't. I wanted an excuse to watch the video anyway. Besides, "I Touch Myself" was a hit because it's a very well-constructed melodic pop song, cheeky and fun, which is why the blunt lyrics don't sound gross. The early arrival of the bridge is clever and Chrissie Amphlett's vocals are both sonorous and seductive. Considering how suggestive it is, the song received little resistance from broadcast censors, who tend to be a little touched themselves at times. As for the video, it's simple yet very alluring, without the pretentious nonsense that shows up in a lot of Madonna videos. I'll take it over the Material Girl's bizarre "Erotic" any day.

Amphlett, by the way, went on to garner critical raves on the musical stage playing Judy Garland opposite Hugh Jackman in the Australian production of *The Boy from Oz*, about the late talented showman Peter Allen. As for guitarist Mark Entee, I just hope he's not still wearing that red getup.

DRIVE

Words and music by Melissa Ferrick
Performed by Melissa Ferrick
Released 2000 (no chart position)

THE FOLLOWING chapter is what's known as a failed experiment.

Allow me to explain. While listening to various women artists one afternoon in search of creepy love ballads, I came across Melissa Ferrick and her lyrically graphic song "Drive." A lesbian singer/songwriter since the early nineties, Ms. Ferrick has amassed a small but loyal following. She works as an independent artist in a musical vein similar to Ani DiFranco, playing eccentric alt-folk songs while busily accompanying herself on guitar. While her songs rarely if ever get any radio airplay, fans know her catalog and seem especially familiar with her song "Drive," judging by the people I heard singing along with it at her shows (I've seen the YouTube videos).

Now comes, as the Bard says, the rub. "Drive" is a song about lesbians for lesbians by a lesbian. I was already out of my element to the power of three. It's also about performing oral sex, and not in a coy hinted-at way. If you can count to five on one hand, you know exactly what "Drive" is about; it's that obvious. Since I honestly don't know anything about the nuances of oral sex between lesbians, I attempted to analyze "Drive" by imagining that two gay women had offered to act out the song's lyrics for me. Upon submitting my critique, an editor sent me the following e-mail (this is not made up).

I have to confess I found your entry for "Drive" creepier than the song itself. Treating lesbians like complete freaks while describing their sexual practices as if you're at the zoo is not, I believe, appropriate for this or any other book. Sorry if I strike you as "politically correct," but this made me see red. If you've shown it to a lesbian and they're OK with it, I'll withdraw my complaint. Otherwise, would you be willing to cut this entry and do a new one on another song? To my mind, it's beyond hope.—Ed.

It was apparent to everyone that my experiment in writing lesbian erotica was a miserable failure and offensive to boot. I was clearly out of my element and had no business describing oral sex between two women based on "Drive." However, since there was no time to do a rewrite, we unfortunately have to print the analysis as originally written, with the offensive parts deleted. Sorry for the confusion.

THE SONG

I'm here inside the lesbian boudoir. Life partners Regina and Cassie have graciously allowed me to observe while they demonstrate something they call **DELETED**. Melissa Ferrick's song "Drive" will play in the background, which it usually does anyway.

The song starts with a slow, loping mix of drums, bass, and acoustic guitar that somewhat resembles Sheryl Crow's "Leaving Las Vegas." The beat here, though, is meant to be suggestive.

"If you want this," Melissa fairly groans, "you're gonna have to ask." She repeats this several times.

I watch as Regina whispers something into Cassie's ear.

"Whatever you want," Melissa hisses, adding that she'll give it to her, give it to her "slowly" until "you're just begging." She'll do that and more, but "you're gonna have to ask."

Regina whispers again in Cassie's ear. Cassie lies back and **DELETED**.

The loping music (basically porn folk) continues as Melissa describes how "your mouth waters . . . fingers trembling."

Following the song's lyrics, Cassie arches her spine and **DELETED**. Regina **DELETED** under Cassie's **DELETED**.

This cues the chorus, "I hold you up and drive you alllll night . . ."

I watch as Regina begins **DELETED** to Cassie. It looks pretty much like how men **DELETED** women except Regina is **DELETED**.

"I hold you up and drive you . . ." Melissa repeats over and over, like a sapphic mantra.

The next stanza has Ms. Ferrick mentioning all the different locations where she'd like to "hold you up," like the kitchen, the shower, the back of a car, inside "your office" during business hours.

Regina takes Cassie and **DELETED DELETED DELETED DELETED DELETED DELETED**.

"I know how you like it," Melissa says with relish (she's yet to sing a note).

Cassie's mouth waters as **DELETED DELETED DELETED** while Regina **DELETED DELETED DELETED DELETED**. Drive, drive, drive . . .

Things become more graphic. Melissa's voice takes on a shaky, eroticized tone as she says how this is where she wants to live, "right here between your hips."

I watch as Regina **DELETED** Cassie while **DELETED DELETED DELETED**.

The vocal track sounds weird, with a second voice added to the mix that sounds as though it's muffled. The lyrics keep repeating over and over, "I'll hold you up and drive you . . ."

Finally, Cassie **DELETED DELETED DELETED** as Regina **DELETED DELETED** and straightens up.

The song fades out, its grinding rhythm still running through my head.

WHY IT'S CREEPY

With its slow, oozing beat and deadpan phone sex vocals, "Drive"'s creepiness comes from the voyeurism that is all over the track, as though you are eavesdropping on an unsuspecting couple. There's nothing self-conscious or artificial about Melissa Ferrick's delivery, and many listeners will get uncomfortable listening to it. "Drive" is not an obscene song, but her performance makes it sound a hundred times more graphic than the lyrics already are. Everyone sounds turned on in the song. Who knows what the drummer was doing to himself? Suffice to say, lesbians and the guys who get off on them will flock to "Drive" the most. Almost everyone else will just feel weird.

As for my trip to the boudoir to watch Regina **DELETED** Cassie, I secretly shot a video and posted it on the Web. Just search under **DELETED DELETED DELETED DELETED** and you'll find it.

PERFECT STORMS

WHISKEY LULLABY

Words and music by Bill Anderson and Jon Randall
Performed by Brad Paisley with Alison Krauss
Released 2003 (No. 3 on U.S. country charts)

AFTER I left college, I spent three ignoble years working as a DJ at an East Texas country music station, a job I was as qualified to do as I am to teach economics to the World Bank. If I learned anything before getting fired, it's that there's nothing more depressing than a depressing country song. I could've filled my previous book of fifty-two most depressing songs with nothing but country tunes alone and had enough left over to dam a river. It's been many years since I've followed country music enough to see who's wearing the Hat nowadays. (All country stars wear the same hat. It's called the Hat.) While searching for a creepy country contender for this volume, I noticed how little things have changed. The wrist-slitting ballads of Alan Jackson today sound exactly like the wrist-slitting ballads of George Strait twenty years ago.

So what led me to the Brad Paisley/Alison Krauss duet recording of "Whiskey Lullaby?" Easy: the damned title. There are a hundred thousand country songs with "Whiskey" in their title and they're all either partying two-steppers or ballads that tempt you to put a pistol in your mouth. "Whiskey Lullaby" is definitely the latter, and besides being fatally depressing, it's also creepy beyond all reckoning. It's one of those pulpy songs in which not enough people can die a horrible death while cramming in every cliche about "the bottle," drinkin' this, drinkin' that, drinkin', drinkin', drinkin'. Everyone's a-drinkin' and a-dyin'. Yee fucking ha and pass the revolver. Brad Paisley and Alison Krauss are as inoffensive as one can get in country music and both are virtuosos on their respective instruments of guitar and fiddle. But while they didn't write "Whiskey Lullaby," I cannot fathom why they chose to record it. Fortunately I managed to score a tape of the recording in the studio and heard the following conversation between Paisley and Kraus, which I've transcribed.

THE SONG

"Howdy, Alison."

"Howdy, Brad. What do you have for us today?"

"A real dandy number called 'Whiskey Lullaby.' It's about a guy whose wife cheats on him and so he gets all piss-drunk 'n' blows his brains out. She feels guilty so she gets all piss-drunk 'n' blows her brains out."

"Wow, that's great. Do they have a dog? Maybe the dog can get all piss-drunk 'n' blow his brains out. Woof!"

"No, there's no dog. But at least the two of them blow their brains out. We got that to work with."

"Then let's get started."

(Acoustic gee-tar picks a chord, cue dobro, cue booze.) "So I'll sing how she put him out like he was a 'midnight cigarette.' He spends the rest of his shattered life tryin' to forget how she broke his heart."

"Wait, Brad, what's a midnight cigarette? Is that any different than a regular one?"

"It's a cigarette that makes you get drunk. See, at this point I'll sing how the rest of us watched as he gets pissed on whiskey tryin' to drink the pain away. But never could get himself drunk enough."

"Wow, I love it when they can't get drunk enough. When do I sing?"

"Right here, when you join me on the chorus. We'll sing how he put the 'bottle to his head and pulled the trigger.'"

"He shoots himself with the bottle?"

"No, with an ole gun. The bottle made him do it. It was the only way he could drink away her memory."

"Really? Wow, I recorded ten songs last week with that line. People sure like to drink away memories a lot."

"Yeah, I've recorded twenty. Anyway, we finish the chorus singin' how we found him face down in his pillow. There's like blood everywhere. It's really creepy and gross."

"Love it! Love it, love it, love it."

"Then we bury him under a willow tree, like we always do with suicides in country songs. The angels show up and sing 'a whiskey lullaby.' It goes like this: 'La la-la la la la laa . . .'"

"So I only sing on the chorus?"

"Heck, no! Why should I have all the fun? You get to kill the woman who broke his heart."

(Acoustic gee-tar interlude, more dobro fills, pick-up truck blows a gasket.)

"Okay, Brad, I'll come in here. I guess everybody's gossipin' about her but they don't know that she blamed herself for him drinkin' and shootin' himself."

"Yeah, so now she starts a-drinkin'. She spends years hoping people don't smell 'the whiskey on her breath.' I love it when they reek of booze."

"Wow, I see that she's drinking *her* pain away now. I was wonderin' when she was gonna start. She still can't get drunk enough, though."

"Now I'll join you on the chorus again only this time she puts the bottle to her head and pulls the trigger. It's the only way she can drink away his memory."

"Wow, that line again. So is her head all splattered too?"

"I reckon so, cuz we find her face down in her pillow. She's holdin' on to his picture. Her brains are splattered all over it. Ain't that great?"

"Golly, that's so tragic and creepy. I love it. We even get to stick her under that same willow tree."

"Yeah, that reminds me. We gotta plant more willows because the bodies are startin' to pile up. Anyways, you and me will take it out from here where the angels show up one last time and sing them 'a whiskey lullaby. La la-la la la la laaa . . .'"

"Aw, Brad, I love this song. Are you sure we can't get the dog to drink away their memories 'n' then blow his brains out? Woof!"

WHY IT'S CREEPY

"Whiskey Lullaby" follows a standard equation that Nashville songwriters have used since the Grand Ole Opry was still a surly teenage Opry: cheatin' + drinkin' + shootin' = ballad. So what makes this double-suicide bourbon ditty creepier than its pathetic brethren? Well, for one, the guy goes off the deep end within the first line of the song just because she broke his heart. You can almost see this chump staggering around waving his Jack Daniels bottle with puke running down his shirt. The thing is, women get cheated on far more often and you don't see them diving into the scotch trough. They just call Alanis Morissette and fill her in. Here, everyone's drinkin' away their pain and memories until they wind up facedown in the pillow following a point-blank pop to the top.

Then there's the damn willow tree. Somewhere there's a willow surrounded by the corpses of the fifty thousand losers who've died in country songs. Just once bury someone under a birch or something. As far as the angels that show up, they're not even singing Schubert's "Ave Maria" or a Gregorian chant. Instead, they're jamming on a "whiskey lullaby," "La la-la la la la laaaa . . ."—which means they either have a twisted sense of humor or will take any request you give them. This song creeps me out no end while laying me out like a medical cadaver. Yee fucking ha.

MUSKRAT LOVE

Words and music by Willis Allan Ramsey
Performed by the Captain and Tennille
Released 1976 (No. 4 in U.S.)

What defines crappy music? Depends who you ask. God knows my college dorm mates hated my anachronistic LP collection. Their eyes glazed over whenever I argued the virtues of Wishbone Ash. They only liked Pink Floyd's *Ummagumma* because they could bong up to it. Now, years later, I'm on the other side of the issue, where the best thing I can say about Akon's "Smack That" is that it probably wasn't *supposed* to suck barbells; it just turned out that way.

Still, every decade offers up a select number of songs that bite the dead crow for literally anyone who hears them. The same question goes through everyone's head: *Who the hell wrote this? And more importantly, why?* While I can understand artists performing an abominable song they wrote, I cannot fathom why they'd *cover* one, especially a song as notoriously awful as "Muskrat Love." This unctuous, creepy ballad about romancing rodents easily ranks as one of the worst songs ever written. Although I'm loath to dredge up the seventies, a decade infamous for awful music, I'd be remiss not to include "Muskrat Love," as it was covered not once but twice by different artists.

"Muskrat Love" was written by Austin singer/songwriter Willis Alan Ramsey, who originally entitled it "Muskrat Candlelight." The soft-rock trio America scored a minor hit in 1971 with a version of the song, which clearly showed it to be a barf banquet. Not everyone got the memo, though, and the softer-pop duo the Captain and Tennille released its own version of "Muskrat Love" in 1976, which went to No. 4 in the U.S.

The Captain and Tennille are married couple Daryl Dragon and Toni Tennille, who were somewhat of a paradox during their seventies heyday, in that both were talented musicians (Tennille is a fine vocalist/pianist who sang backup on Pink Floyd's *The Wall*, while Dragon is a superlative keyboard player) who released some of the worst songs ever recorded. When they weren't writing them, they were finding them elsewhere. ("Attention, songwriters: please send us the most useless tripe you've ever written. You won't regret it.") They struck gold in 1975 with Neil Sedaka's "Love Will Keep Us Together" and went on to chart several more releases, including their soporific version of the cheese-chewing (really! see the lyrics!) "Muskrat Love."

THE SONG

While doing research for "Muskrat Love," I was invariably led to muskrats, a subject I knew nothing about save having worked for a few in the past. Their scientific name is *Ondatra zibethicus* (the song's is *Sonicus regurgivomitus*). Muskrats are very large rat cousins that live in swamps, breed copiously, and are considered a nuisance because they burrow into levees and earthen dams. They also have unique nostrils shaped like a 7 that allow them to recirculate oxygen while breathing so they can stay underwater for fifteen minutes at a time. (If you think you're bored now, wait till you read about the song.)

The Captain and Tennille's version of "Muskrat Love" opens with the Captain laying down a mush of arpeggios on a woozy electric piano that sounds like a vibraphone dipped in cake batter. Meanwhile, Tennille sets up the romantic scene of two muskrats out on the town, complete with candlelight and some earthen dam burrowing. Their names are Muskrat Susie and Muskrat Sam, a nomenclature that, if universally applied, would result in Mouse Mickey and Duck Donald. Susie and Sam, we learn, are doing the jitterbug in muskrat land, a magical place where waterborne rodents perform Second World War–era dances and one pill makes you larger, one pill makes you small. Also, while they "shimmy," we find out Sammy's "so skinny," perhaps the dumbest rhyme ever concocted.

The chorus consists of Sam and Susie whirling, twirling, and tangoing (the jitterbug being passé now), which sets up the next bad rhyme, where they're "singin' and jingin' the jango." For the record, neither "jinging" nor "jango" can be found in the dictionary, so I'm not sure what a jango looks like, let alone how the hell you jing one. Regardless, the end result is "Muskrat Love."

The next stanza features the culinary habits of our two muskrats, namely bacon nibbling and cheese chewing. The common muskrat eats frogs, clams, water plants, and crayfish. Bacon and cheese can only be found at muskrat-owned Burger King franchises. Anyway, during this cheesy bacon fest, Sam proposes to Susie, asking for her paw in marriage. Susie happily agrees and some hot nasty muskrat action takes place. He tickles her fancy, rubs her toes, maybe even jings her jango for all we care. They go "muzzle to muzzle" and this sends Susie into a giggling fit, which the the Captain and Tennille replicate by making bizarre twittering noises with a synthesizer. Evidently, tittering muskrats sound like a shortwave radio tuning in Ecuador.

After a final spin through the chorus of twirling tangoing and jango jinging, Sam and Susie fall hopelessly into "muskrat love," leading to muskrat marriage, muskrat mistresses, muskrat separation, and muskrat divorce. They swim off together into the sunset to tell other muskrats the news.

WHY IT'S CREEPY

Remember the universal crappy song question: "Who the hell wrote this? And more importantly, why?" This has plagued many a hater of "Muskrat Love" (that being anyone who's ever heard it), especially the latter part. The typical muskrat female can produce up to twenty-four muskrat-ettes during her lifetime, which would suggest that "Muskrat Love" is a very fruitful concept. It's just that I'd rather learn about it from one of the nature documentaries on television than from the Captain and Tennille. Besides, why would anyone write a love song about the courting rituals of marsh-dwelling fauna? Were wildebeests already taken? Why do these two cheese-eating swamp bunnies need to jing the jango in Muskrat Land? The song's overly cutesy nature is so excessive that even Motorhead couldn't overcome it, and when you have the Captain and Tennille oozing through the muskrat muck, you can feel the sap flowing up your spine.

BEN

Words and music by Don Black and Walter Scharf
Performed by Michael Jackson
Released 1972 (No. 1 in U.S., No. 7 in UK)

DEPENDING ON who you are, Michael Jackson is either a preternaturally talented singer, dancer, and songwriter with the bestselling album of all time (*Thriller*, natch) or a talcum-colored freak with a detachable nose, Peter Pan obsession, and bankroll the size of Wyoming (although it's now about as big as my parents' garden shed). While I can see both sides, for me the degree to which he imploded his career is another talent unto itself. If the King of Pop has accomplished anything, it's showing how to go from being the biggest performer in the world to the punch line to every sick joke involving children and zoo animals. In the good old days, you only made fun of the one glove.

Jackson has basically had two careers: young member of a successful pop group and mega-selling solo artist. The latter has all but eclipsed his early work with the Jackson 5, which for my money was the best teenage music act of all time. While his first solo release was the single "Got to Be There," it was the bizarre "Ben" that gave Jackson his first No. 1 hit. Yes, kids, before "Billie Jean," "Thriller," "Beat It" and that terrible duet with Sir Paul, there was "Ben," and it deserves inclusion to our creepy love song hall of fame because it's a love ballad to a rat.

"Ben" is the theme song to the 1972 film of the same name, an inferior sequel to the 1971 cult horror film *Willard* about a teased social misfit who befriends rats and trains them to kill his tormentors. In the movie *Ben*, a lonely little boy finds the rat leader Ben and its killer pack living inside his house, and dispatches them on bullies at his school (nowadays kids use a

9mm for that). The film ends with the rat colony being destroyed, although Ben escapes, crawling back to the boy's house. As the kid nurses him to life, the rat peers menacingly at the camera, plotting his revenge. The credits roll and the song kicks in, probably not the revenge he had in mind.

THE SONG

His incisors clotted with human flesh, an injured and burned Ben rests on a towel on top of a table as the boy applies iodine to his cuts. Ben thinks, "Man, this sucks. My crew's dead, my fur's scorched, and this little shit in the plaid pants is sticking me with a Q-tip soaked in iodine. How could it get any worse?" Suddenly, a melancholy intro of acoustic guitar arpeggios and drop-dead bass wafts in, followed by an impossibly high tenor voice that will never experience puberty. "Ben," the voice warbles, "the two of us need look no morrre . . ."—adding how they've both finally found what they're looking for (unlikely, unless it's the half-gnawed face of a dead sewer worker). We learn that neither of them will ever be alone. Michael now has a friend to call his own while Ben has "got a friend in me."

As Ben clamps his paws over his ears, he's told how he's spent most of his scabies-ridden life running here and there, never being wanted by anyone because, well, he's a rat. But not to worry, Ben, if you don't like what you see when you "look behind," you always have a place to go: the Jackson estate, to be with Michael and his forty-eight brothers and sisters (if he can live with Latoya, he can live with a rat).

The song's bridge is particularly cloying. "I used to say 'I' and 'me,'" Ben hears Michael sing, but now it's "us" and "we." *What's with the grammar lesson?* he thinks. *Why am I being assaulted with pronouns? And who the hell are those background singers? They sound like the cleaning crew.*

The final verse has the voice reminding Ben how most people would run away from him screaming, only to return with a bat and smash him to a bloody pulp (OK, it doesn't say that exactly, but that's what I'd do). He doesn't listen to them, Michael insists, adding how people don't see carnivorous vermin the same way he does. Everyone should have "a friend like Ben." The music ends quietly and Ben does the only logical thing he can think of: he leaps on the kid and chews a hole in his neck.

WHY IT'S CREEPY

Though dated and sappy, there is nothing disturbing about the song itself. The melody is pleasant and Jackson's vocal is quite impressive considering he was only thirteen at the time (although the background singers really are terrible). It's only when you realize he's singing to a man-eating rat that "Ben" veers off into the bad camp arena. It's probable that most teenage fans who bought the single never knew this, since the film *Ben* wasn't a hit.

Now, let's jump ahead thirty-five years to an era when the phrase "a Michael Jackson song" has an entirely different meaning to it. "Ben" is an example of a creepy love song that becomes creepier when you disregard the thing that made it creepy to begin with. In other words, switch the rat with a ten-year-old boy named Ben. See what I mean? Of the thousands of boys whose clueless parents shoved them into Jackson's orbit over the years, the odds are that a few of them were named Ben.

On a given day, Ben spends the day at Neverland Ranch riding the choo-choo, feeding the llamas, and playing charades with Bubbles the chimp. Now, it's nighttime. Ben and Michael are tucked away in the master bedroom watching a DVD of *Charlie and the Chocolate Factory* starring Johnny Depp. Ben sips hot cocoa while Jackson guzzles merlot. He watches Depp, thinking, "Man, that Willy Wonka guy sure looks familiar . . ."

The movie now over, Jackson turns to Ben, adjusts his wig, smiles, and sings softly, "Ben, the two of us need look no morrre . . ."

Ben is currently settling for $20 million.

(YOU'RE) HAVING MY BABY

Words and music by Paul Anka
Performed by Paul Anka (with Odia Coates)
Released 1974 (No. 1 in U.S., No. 6 in UK)

FOR ME, the Hangover 1970s will always be the mother lode where one can find hit songs that sucked worse than anything could possibly suck. If you need evidence of the horrors of cocaine, look no further than the Grammy awards and the winners back then: Debby Boone, Chuck Mangione, Starland Vocal Band, Leo Sayer, Silver Connection, Donna Summer, Anne Murray, Kenny Rogers, Glen Campbell, and other artists who I've spent the past thirty years purging from my memory. Trophies were showered on execrable releases like "You Light Up My Life" and "Rhinestone Cowboy," while the Clash and Talking Heads were roundly ignored.

This rant has a purpose, as it brings us to Paul Anka's "(You're) Having My Baby." Offensive beyond the pale, this vile lounge ballad reached No. 1 in 1974 (a banner year for bad hit records) and has gone on to becomee one of the worst songs ever recorded, even worse than "Muskrat Love." Oddly enough, "Having My Baby" was Anka's "comeback" after he failed to score a hit single since 1959's "Lonely Boy." Born in Canada in 1941, Paul Anka was a fifties teenage idol before settling into a respected career as a Vegas crooner like his contemporaries Bobby Darin and Wayne Newton. While uncool to the point of terminally tepid, Anka is a seasoned musician/arranger who writes most of his own material, with over nine hundred songs to his credit. That said, there isn't enough penance in the world he can do to make up for the hideousness of "(You're) Having My Baby," or enough conspiracy theories to explain how this song got played on the radio.

Because "Having My Baby" is so egregiously creepy, I knew I'd have to include it in this book. Of course, this meant having to listen to the damned thing, but such tortures come with the territory, so I diligently set out to do a thorough analysis of "(You're) Having My Baby" and write a comprehensive essay. Then a strange thing happened—and I'm not making this up.

I couldn't find the song.

Seriously, it was nowhere to be found. My subscription music site Rhapsody didn't have it. Napster didn't have it. The mega warehouse record store near me didn't have it. Illegal file-sharing Web sites like (**name deleted**) and (**name deleted**) didn't have it. Even iTunes didn't offer "Having My Baby." Oh, it had other songs available for purchase from *Paul Anka's Greatest Hits*, but not "Having My Baby." Never mind stealing, I wasn't even allowed to buy it.

Undaunted, I surfed the Web, searching like a masochistic Magellan for any trace of an audio file of "Having My Baby." Potential links led me to derelict pages, broken connections, and some guy asking for money so he could keep his Web site operating. The only things I could find were the lyrics and a karaoke instrumental track of the song, as if there's a demand for one.

It's a telling sign when a former No. 1 hit record becomes impossible to find. Apparently some omnipresent music censor has issued a decree by which nobody is allowed to possess a copy of "Having My Baby" for fear of it actually being played. I considered dropping the song from the book but realized I'd be derelict in my duty to bring classic crap to the masses. So I only had one option left: recall the song from memory.

THE SONG

As I drift back to summer 1974, I'm a kid swimming at the Rothschild municipal pool in Wisconsin. A bunch of us are doing cannonballs off the diving board for the sole purpose of getting the lifeguards wet so they can call us little assholes and kick us out. An FM transistor radio tuned to WIFC, the local Top 40 station, is being piped through a tiny outdoor PA speaker. There are some cool songs out by War and Billy Preston, and Elton John's new single "Someone Saved My Life Tonight." All seems fine in the world when suddenly a syrupy MOR song interrupts our splashing, complete with strings, chirping flute, and cloying electric piano. After four, no wait, eight bars of this velvety mush, an unfamiliar voice that's too low for tenor and too high for baritone (let's call it a tene-bone) slides its way to the front. "You're having my baby," it croons disgustingly, adding that it's a lovely way of saying "how much you love me." While farting bubbles in the blue water, my friends and I pause and gaze at each other perplexed. "You're having my baby," the voice repeats, commending someone for "thinking of me." He can see the baby's glowing face in her eyes, too. Although we're young and oblivious to most of life's darker aspects, we still ponder the greater question: "What the fuck is this shit?"

The chorus is the same as the verse section, except there's a black female singer singing along. "I love what it's doin' to ya," the tene-bone remarks, including morning sickness, constipation, and mood swings.

Shuddering, we head for the pool's edge to bang the water out of our ears. Ohmigod, we think, he's talking about the seed growing inside her. He sees the need showing on her face. Who is this freaking guy? He makes John Denver sound like Black Sabbath.

Our prepubescent minds are learning that she didn't have to keep the baby. She could've swept it away and out of her life. But no, she wouldn't do it because she loves what's "goin' through me" and so (once again) she's having his baby. I hear the flute trills, the buried strings, the music box keyboard, the gospel vocalist who was somehow forced to duet with the tene-bone so he could wail about knocking her up. There may have been a key change towards the end, I'm not sure. All I know is that infernal chorus will always be stuck in my mind.

Finally the song ends, and the announcer says we've just heard the new single by Paul Anka (who?) which is currently racing up the charts. And now here's the latest from Olivia Newton John! My friend Dave and I pick up our towels and start strangling each other.

WHY IT'S CREEPY

The reputation of "(You're) Having My Baby" has long preceded it, and the song has become part of the cultural lexicon that defines repellent music. The repetitious chorus, the graphic yet syrupy lyrics, the sperm imagery, the abortion reference, it's all there. It's one of those rare songs that's so creepy, it has to be heard to be believed while being the last thing in the world you'd ever want to listen to. Still, I was sickly astonished that I recalled it so vividly, especially after going through the lyrics.

As a coda to my dysfunctional flashback, WIFC was the kind of ass-wipe station that played every song in the Top 10 a zillion times a day, which meant this obnoxious baby song was probably going to torment us for a while. Sure enough, the remainder of my summer of '74 at the pool was ruined because every time I went for an afternoon dip, that swine Anka came on the PA speaker to remind me that he banged some chick and got his seed inside her. If it hadn't been for Edgar Winter's "Frankenstein," I never would've survived.

DON'T STOP SWAYING

Words and music by Sophie B. Hawkins
Performed by Sophie B. Hawkins
Released 1992 (no chart position)

You're probably familiar with the concept of a Sadie Hawkins Dance. It's like any other school dance except that girls invite the boys to go along with them. But imagine they've renamed it a Sophie Hawkins Dance. In order to attend, the girls must ask their brothers to be their date. They'll be required to slow-dance together under the mirror ball then fornicate afterwards in the backseat of a car. If they don't have a brother, a sister can substitute. If they have no siblings, they can't attend.

Welcome to the creepiest and worst love song ever written, Sophie B. Hawkins' "Don't Stop Swaying." Once you hear it you Won't Stop Barfing Until She Stops Singing. If there's a love song creepier than this, I can't imagine it, because you'd have to be one sick puppy to write a tune sicker than "Don't Stop Swaying" and do it *unintentionally*. The song confirms my theory that it's the woefully misguided, not the willfully perverse, who create the worst of the worst. None of the necrophilia songs included in this book made it as Perfect Storms, because they're supposed to be shocking. "Don't Stop Swaying" is a serious love song by someone who thinks confession is an Olympic event. It's also nothing less than a celebratory anthem to incest, one that's even creepier than "Incestuous Love."

Sophie B. Hawkins was a member of the CHAI movement who scored a Top 10 hit in 1992 with "Damn, I Wish I Was Your Lover" followed by "As I Lay Me Down" two years later. A graduate of the Manhattan School of Music, Hawkins is a skilled multi-instrumentalist with a warm voice and sultry stage presence (call me shallow, I think she's pretty hot). Like her contemporary Paula Cole, Hawkins also shares waaaay too much information about her quirks, obsessions, and personal life in her songs. A self-proclaimed "omnisexual," there seemingly isn't a species of flora or fauna that she won't give her phone number to. One only needs to hear tracks like "Your Tongue Like the Sun in My Mouth" to wonder if her therapist takes steroids just to keep up with her. With "Don't Stop Swaying," though, you're dealing with a whole different level of ugliness.

THE SONG

I knew I was in trouble even before I listened to "Don't Stop Swaying." The lyrics alone gave me a Freudian migraine and the track indicated it was almost six minutes long. When I started the song, it creeped me out right away because I had it on headphones and the first thing I heard was Hawkins whispering something like "looks good, put it in your hair" or "cooks food, good with angel hair," something like that, followed by those chimes you hear in films about children who kill their parents with pitchforks. Next, various percussion instruments dribble into the mix while a fretless bass and New Age synth lay down a bed of contemplative fog. We're now ready to audition for *Flowers in the Attic*. "I saw you there," Hawkins begins while adding how all she ever wanted was to "start with you." Great, her first erotic fantasy is to get into bed with her brother. No wonder he keeps yelling at her to stay out of his room. It was hard to convince him, mind you, probably the most difficult "thing I ever had to do." But he came around, oh, you betcha. They made a deal: she'll do his homework for him if he'll go down on her like a deer at a salt lick.

"Yo brother," she calls to him while renewing her subscription to *I Have Issues Weekly*. She thanks him for hearing her while she was "banging on the big drums" for his love, making it the only time a timpani's been used for foreplay.

Eventually she gets him between the sheets, where she makes him call her baby and act like her best friend (those omnisexuals sure know how to party). Finally, he asks her what she likes, which takes us to the creepy chorus. "Don't stop swaying, baby," she tells him needlessly since he's probably too drunk not to sway. There's the obligatory references to souls being soothed, searches ceased, she sells seashells by the seashore, etc. She's "lost in the rhythm" and it "stops hurting." Well, maybe for you. I'm in serious pain right now.

Now it's the brother's turn. He calls to her, thanking her for hearing him while he was "singing in the rain" for love. Quick, let's run over to Gene Kelly's grave and listen to him spin. He recalls how she took him unaware and now the "time is ripe." She asks him what he likes, bringing us back to the chorus. So now we have two inbreeding dweebs who can't stop their swaying, soothing their souls, or ceasing their searches. And you thought *your* family was messed up.

At this point, we're three minutes into the song with the wash of synth pads still hovering over everything like a cloud with a head injury. It should end here, but suddenly the most awful thing that could ever happen to a song happens in this song. Hawkins starts *talking*. Not rapping, yelling, or sermonizing, just talking. What's this, the Doors? At least Jim Morrison had an excuse; he was wasted when he rambled about lizards and Indians. What's she talking about?

Hansel and Gretel.

So now we know who the incestuous siblings are that won't stop swaying. In the original Grimm's fairy tale, an evil witch tries to bake them in her oven but they manage to cook her instead. But now Sophie B. Hawkins has come in with a swell idea for a rewrite. Instead of a parable about bravery and family ties, let's have them get the hots for each other and boff in the forest. They've fallen in love, she tells us in a voice that sounds as though she's teaching yoga to a dying swan. They kiss, "traveling like heat through each other . . ." (Oh, for fuck's sake.) Hawkins has Hans and Gret living in the forest for the rest of their lives, peacefully screwing, before ending with the appalling declaration, "This is what they want. This is who they are." The song fades after nearly six minutes of this jaw-dropping crapola.

WHY IT'S CREEPY

When I have to confront something like "Don't Stop Swaying," my first inclination is to get bombed out of my skull. But I approached the song with a clear head in order to give it a fair hearing, and still came away needing a shower and some Thorazine. Everything about "Don't Stop Swaying" is wrong, including its New Age conceit, gaseous keyboard bed, badly sung vocals (she employs the annoying technique of whispering along with her singing), and self-indulgent endorsement of a brother and sister doing the nasty. I'm certain Hawkins has a long, convoluted explanation as to why she wrote this song and what her intentions were. She'll probably insist that it's not an endorsement of incest but rather a metaphorical examination of spiritual love, symbiosis, a balanced chakra, harmonic convergence. Or maybe she's just nuts.

Hawkins has all the musical talent, good looks, and artistic attributes to be a force in the entertainment industry, except the ability to put the brakes on whatever the hell runs through her mind like Elektra taking a leap into Niagara Falls. Although I'm no fan of the major labels, I'm convinced that her I-must-reveal-everything style of songwriting is why they all switched over to Britney, Christina, and the rest of the Mouseketeer spawn. Seriously, which one would you rather hang out with, Jessica Simpson in her Daisy Dukes or a woman who fantasizes about siblings screwing each other in a German fairy tale?

HONORABLE MENTIONS, PLUS THE FUTURE

I'M OFTEN asked what it takes to write books like this one. When putting songs in order, what makes the 37th creepiest love song more creepy than the 38th or 39th? Why did I leave out such-and-such? And what *almost* made the list?

For pure narcissism, one runner-up was the appalling hip-hop hit "This Is Why I'm Hot" by the rapper MIMS, in which he answers a question that nobody ever asked him. The song was all over the radio during early 2007, with a backing track that resembles a drum machine with a weak battery mixed with defective sonar. The biggest reason "This Is Why I'm Hot" didn't make the final list is because there's nothing to write about. Half of the lyrics are:

> *This is why I'm hot, this is why I'm hot,*
> *This is why, this is why, this is why I'm hot*
> (repeat until sun explodes)

The reason why he's hot is because he's "fly," that nifty slang adjective for being fabulous. Accordingly, MIMS is the only person in the world who's achieved flydom, and has anointed himself lord of the flies. As for the rest of us, we ain't fly cuz we not. There's a bunch of hoary cliches about "pimps," "bitches," "niggas," tired stuff that Snoop Dogg did ten years ago. It's less a song than a crap collage and is destined for consignment to the inferno of hated one-hit wonders.

One song that I considered in the obsessive category was the classic 1970 Eric Clapton hit "Layla," written during his Derek and the Dominos phase. The song is notorious for being an anguished love note to George Harrison's then-wife, model Patty Boyd. Clapton had fallen in love with her and went so far as to tell his friend Harrison about it. In an odd gesture of altruism, Harrison stepped aside and allowed Boyd to flee into Clapton's arms. The two married in 1974 only to divorce eleven years later. Clapton still performs "Layla" in concert, having emotionally distanced himself from it so much that it's just another guitar workout. The original recording still holds up nicely, though, and Clapton's impassioned vocal remains intact. Adding to the song's creepy subtext is the tragic coda of drummer Jim Gordon, who composed and played the striking piano music that closes "Layla." A legendary session drummer who played on hundreds of hit recordings, Gordon later became afflicted with paranoid schizophrenia and began hearing voices in his head. In 1983 he killed his own mother, bludgeoning her with an axe, and was sentenced to sixteen years to life in prison. He remains incarcerated.

Beyoncé's over-the-top (and bottom) title cut from her 2003 album *Dangerously in Love* was a close contender for the Touch Me, I'm Sick category. I saw Ms. Knowles banshee-wail this seismic ballad on a televised awards show a few years ago and wondered why the stage lights didn't come crashing down on her. Featuring stiff programmed rhythms and an ADD choir that can't make up its mind where to come in, the song features yet another example of overblown aquatic imagery. Beyoncé calls him her "raindrop" while she's the "sea." If one lone raindrop affects her ocean level that much, I'm assuming it's a well-hung raindrop. Still, I can't imagine who'd want to hear that someone is "dangerously" in love with them; that adverb tends to scare people away no matter how it's used ("I'll drive you to work . . . dangerously"). Beyoncé goes so far as to tell the guy she can see herself having his child and being his wife (in that order). Talk about pressure. While Beyoncé hits nearly a 10 on the gospel Richter scale, the song's disingenuous nature keeps it from being a total creep-fest. I seriously doubt she gets this gaga over anyone, Jay-Z or otherwise, which makes it just another slick ballad of rote emotionalism.

Other runners-up included Alan O'Day's creepily awful "Undercover Angel," a No. 1 hit in 1977 and yet another misuse of a celestial being. O'Day was a songwriter who wrote the nutso Helen Reddy hit "Angie Baby," about a crazy girl living at home who lets a neighbor boy climb into her bedroom so she can shrink him down by playing the radio, or something like that. "Undercover Angel," though, is plain terrible, an up-tempo song about a lonely guy who discovers a woman has magically materialized in his bed, begging him to sleep with her. It's the first time an angel gets cast as an easy lay. The angel then vanishes, urging the man to find the "right" lover, where he'll find her again. The song's chorus includes the line of how he's never had a dream that "makes sweet love to me." There are too many easy comebacks to this phrase, so I'll just ignore it. "Undercover Angel" is yet another example of the bankruptcy of seventies music.

For good-creepy songs, there was Janis Joplin's wrenching "Piece of My Heart," and the widely misunderstood "One" by U2 and "The One I Love" by REM, both of them angry kiss-off songs that many listeners consider anthems of comfort. Green Day's "Good Riddance (Time of Your Life)" has become a popular song at weddings and proms with people who likewise don't pay attention to the lyrics and choose to ignore half the song's title. UK pop singer Lily Allen's maliciously cheery hit "Smile" appeared too late for consideration, although it would've made a great candidate. Hearing this petite little thing sharpening her knives over an errant boyfriend while the song's ska-light music plays behind her makes it one of the more memorable revenge songs of recent years.

As for the future of creepy love songs, I foresee a bright one for both the good and the bad. As subtlety and innuendo have become as passé as eight-track tapes, songwriters really have no choice but to spill everything in the most graphic ways imaginable. The fact that people still play "Every Breath You Take" at weddings, "The One I Love" at proms, and "Good

Riddance (Time of Your Life)" at funerals is just proof that we don't listen to lyrics any more, cannot comprehend messages, and are incapable of interpreting even the most basic symbolism. We need everything explained to us as though it were instructions to assembling a desk. Love has no mystery left, no privacy, no discretion. Love's worth nothing unless it looks good on camera or sells magazines. It must be purchased, customized, color-coordinated, choreographed, scored, and put out with a suitable publicity campaign behind it. This is why today's love songs need to push everything to the highest level, leaving lyrical subtleties behind to gather dust among old Sinatra records. As it's quite easy to find songs about incest and necrophilia today, nothing's off-limits. Why write about a crush on the girl next door when we can love corpses, blood relatives, the devil, and the occasional farm animal?

Seriously, one of the greatest and most passionate love songs I've heard during the last thirty-plus years is Queen's "I'm in Love with My Car," which offers more real devotion than a thousand Mariah ballads. For those unfamiliar with it, though, "I'm in Love with My Car" is about a guy who's in love with his car. That's just in case you're thinking of playing it at your wedding.

TOUCH ME, I'M SICK
THE FINAL COUNTDOWN

52. Your Body Is a Wonderland/John Mayer
51. Invisible/Clay Aiken
50. My Heart Belongs to Daddy/Julie London
49. Making Love Out of Nothing at All/Air Supply
48. To Know Him Is to Love Him/The Teddy Bears
47. My Boy Lollipop/Millie
46. Butterfly Kisses/Bob Carlisle
45. Obsession/Animotion
44. Thank Heaven for Little Girls/Maurice Chevalier
43. Pieces of Me/Ashlee Simpson
42. Me and My Old Lady/The Offspring
41. Pride and Joy/Coverdale-Page
40. Butterfly/Weezer
39. Break Me/Jewel
38. Run for Your Life/The Beatles
37. Afternoon Delight/Starland Vocal Band
36. Creep/Radiohead
35. I Touch Myself/Divinyls
34. You're Beautiful/James Blunt
33. You're All I Need/Motley Crue
32. Butterfly/Mariah Carey
31. Father Figure/George Michael
30. Come to My Window/Melissa Etheridge
29. Pretty When You Cry/VAST
28. Fergalicious/Fergie
27. Baby Love/Joan Osborne
26. I've Never Been to Me/Charlene
25. Code Blue/TSOL
24. Angels Fuck/Jack Off Jill

23. Jenny from the Block/Jennifer Lopez
22. Butterfly/Candlebox
21. Vermilion & Vermilion Pt. 2/Slipknot
20. Incestuous Love (Amours Incestueuses)/Marc Almond
19. Where the Wild Roses Grow/Nick Cave with Kylie Minogue
18. I'm Not in Love/10cc
17. Marry Me (Heirate Mich)/Rammstein
16. Dirrty/Christina Aguilera
15. Alive/Pearl Jam
14. Feelin' Love/Paula Cole
13. Lose Control/Kevin Federline
12. Drive/Melissa Ferrick
11. There Is a Light That Never Goes Out/The Smiths
10. Every Breath You Take/The Police
9. Possession/Sarah McLachlan
8. You Oughta Know/Alanis Morissette
7. I Am Stretched on Your Grave/Sinéad O'Connor
6. Stan/Eminem
5. Ben/Michael Jackson
4. Whiskey Lullaby/Brad Paisley with Alison Krauss
3. Muskrat Love/The Captain and Tennille
2. (You're) Having My Baby/Paul Anka
1. Don't Stop Swaying/Sophie B. Hawkins

SONG CREDITS